IMPERIAL GORKHA :

An Account of Gorkhali Rule in Kumaun (1791—1815)

Mahesh C. Regmi

Adroit Publishers
DELHI

IMPERIAL GORKHA

Ist Edition : 1999
ISBN 81-87392-02-9

Published by :
Adroit Publishers
C-8/2, Yamuna Vihar,
Delhi - 110053

Laser Typesetting by :
Stylish Laser Typesetter
Delhi

Printed at :
Roshan offset
Delhi.

A Golden Jubilee Gift
for
MANADEVI

Acknowledgements

This study has been possible only because I have been given access to the archival records in the possession of the Records Division of the Department of Land Revenue in the Ministry of Finance of His Majesty's Government of Nepal. It is, therefore, a pleasure to record my gratitude to the then Finance Minister, Rishikesh Shah, who arranged official permission for me to have transcriptions of the materials I needed. I am also indebted to the late Shanker M. Amatya and Krishna M. Arjyal, and their teams, who did superb work in helping me select and transcribe records that were relevant to the subjects of my research and writing at different times. The concerned officials of the Department, who helped locate documents and provided space and other facilities, also deserve thanks, although they are too numerous to be individually mentioned.

I am also grateful to Dr. Joanna Pfaff-Czarnecka for stimulating albeit intermittent conversations which helped me devise the conceptual framework of this study. Kurt Meyer, Pamela Deuel, Stephen J. Keeling, and Pratyoush Onta gave ideas and suggestions which have greatly improved both the content and the style within the limits of my own capability. Thanks are due to Suresh Regmi for his invaluable assistance in finalizing the text and preparing it for publication. Nor can I forget the enthusiasm with which Ravi Regmi helped in the different stages of the work. I only regret that I have not been able to take more advantage of all this help and cooperation.

Mahesh C. Regmi

Prologue

In the wide ocean upon which we venture, the possible ways and directions are many; and the same studies which have served for this work might easily in other hands not only receive a wholly different treatment and application, but lead also to essentially different conclusions. Such, indeed, is the importance of the subject that it still calls for fresh investigation, and may be studied with advantage from the most varied points of view. Meanwhile, we are content if a patient hearing is granted us, and if this book be taken and judged as a whole.

J. Burckhardt (1818-97)[1]

By the early years of the 19th century, the Gorkhali rulers had succeeded in bringing under their control the Himalayan region from the Tista river in the east to the Sutlej river in the west. In the process of expansion, nearly 50 principalities were annexed and their rulers deposed. The small hill state of Gorkha, with its new capital in Kathmandu, emerged as an Empire, uniting many territories and people under Gorkhali rule. My earlier volume on the imperial period, *Kings and Political Leaders of the Gorkhali Empire, 1768-1814*,[2] explained the social and economic motivations for the creation of the Gorkhali Empire. The present volume is a sequel to that study. It discusses the policies and programmes followed by the Gorkhali rulers

1. J. Burckhardt, *The Civilization of the Renaissance in Italy*, trans. by S.G.C. Middlemore, 1944, p. 1, cited in John B. Morrall, *The Medieval Imprint*, 1967, p. 8.
2. Mahesh C. Regmi, *Kings and Political Leaders of the Gorkhali Empire, 1768-1814*, 1995.

to control and administer the provinces of that Empire. The causal approach (why it happened) followed in *Kings and Political Leaders* is here supplemented by a functional approach (how it functioned). The questions raised in this volume are as follows: What were the instruments of imperial control over the subjugated territories and populations ? How did these instruments work in actual practice ? Finally, how did the imperial controls affect the life of the common people ?

For this study, I have chosen the province of Kumaun, which is now a part of the territories of the Indian Union. The choice needs an explanation. In the first place, it keeps the study within manageable limits. Secondly, among the territories conquered and administered by the Gorkhali rulers outside the boundaries of modern Nepal, Gorkhali rule was the longest in Kumaun, a quarter-century between 1791 and 1815. Finally, I have been able to study a mass of unpublished official Nepali documents which had never been available to scholars and so present a virgin field for research. Most of these documents have been transcribed from the official copies in the possession of the Department of Land Revenue in the Ministry of Finance of His Majesty's Government. I have about 100 volumes of copies of these documents in my collection, which I have designated as the *Regmi Research Collection (RRC)*.

My use of the term *Gorkhali state* needs an explanation. I have chosen to use this term to describe the political entity that emerged from the territorial expansion of the State of Gorkha during the latter part of the 18th and the early years of the 19th century. The capital of that State was shifted from Gorkha to Kathmandu in 1768, but the use of the term Gorkhali State (*Gorkha Raj*) was not given up. The term *Nepal* then denoted only the valley of Kathmandu.[3] The Gorkhali

3. Regulations for the Bheri-Jamuna region, Kartik badi 2, 1867 (October 1810), Regmi Research Collection (RRC), Vol. 39, p. 456. This document refers to "troops travelling between Nepal

(Contd.)

State was based on the concept of *dhungo*, literally a stone, but used as a metaphor to denote the state.[4] The concept implied that the Gorkhali state was a permanent entity that transcended the person of the ruler. In other words, allegiance to the state superseded personal loyalty to the ruler. The concept found its practical application in the principle of territorial integrity, an essential attribute of a state in the modern sense.

I have described the Gorkhali State of the late 18th and early 19th centuries as an Empire. To those who are acquainted with such historical empires as the Mughal Empire and the British Empire, the use of the term to denote the Gorkhali state may seem presumptuous. However, it is the nature of the control, rather than its extent, that determines whether or not a state is an empire. The term is used to describe *a state of vast size composed of more or less distinct national units and subject to a single centralized will...*[5] That is to say, it denotes *an expansionist attempt or policy by one state or some of its citizens to influence, exploit, and dominate the people of another, usually weaker, country by overt or covert*

---

and the front". A royal order of August 1811 describes the valley of Kathmandu as "*Nepal Khalta*" (Confirmation of land grants in the region east of Sindhu-Sanga, Bhadra sudi 5, 1868. (August 1811), *RRC*, Vol. 40, p. 289) and gives its boundaries as west of Sanga and east of Bhimdhunga and Thankot; "Adalko" (On Discipline) in Gorkhapatra Chhapakhana: *Muluki Ain* (Legal Code) 2012 (1955), sec. 29, pt. 5, p. 15. This law mentions "*Gorkha Raj*".

4. One of the earliest references to the term in this sense is contained in"Shri 5 Prithvinarayan Shahale Pandita Rajivalochanalai Pathayeko Patra" (A letter sent by King Prithivi Narayan Shah to Pandit Rajivalochana), Magh Badi 9, 1802 (January 19, 1746), in Nayaraj Pant. *et. al*, *Shri 5 Prithvinarayan Shahako Upadesh* (Teachings of King Prithvi Narayan Shah), pt. 3, pp. 932-38).

5. Moritz Julius Bonn, "Imperialism", in *Encyclopaedia of the Social Sciences*, New York, 1963, Vols. VII-VIII, p. 613.

political, military and economic and cultural means.[6] This is an accurate description of the relationship between the Gorkhali Empire and the province of Kumaun.

The imperialist nature of the relationship between the Gorkhali state and the province of Kumaun raises some new questions. At what point did the Gorkhali state assume the form of an empire ? In *Kings and Political Leaders*, I had drawn a distinction between the heartland and the provinces of the Gorkhali Empire, but there was no clear line of demarcation between the two. Indeed, it is difficult to define them in geographical terms. For the purpose of this study, they may be defined in terms of the residence of the political and administrative leaders of the Gorkhali State. Since that leadership was almost wholly restricted to select communities and families from the hill state of Gorkha, the heartland may be defined as encompassing the regions where those communities and families resided. In practical terms, therefore, the Gorkhali heartland was mainly comprised of areas inhabited by *Thakuris, Chhetris, Brahmins, and Khawas*, and such ethnic communities as *Magar* and *Gurung* in Gorkha and other territories in the Trishuli-Marsyangdi region. While Gorkha furnished the political leaders of the Gorkhali state, the other territories furnished a part of the administrative and military personnel. But such personnel only occupied the middle echelons of the Gorkhali establishment and were seldom given any decision-making role. The capital of the Gorkhali State was shifted to Kathmandu after it was conquered by the Gorkhalis in 1768. But Kathmandu itself made hardly any contribution to the Gorkhali leadership, administration, and army. Almost all the families that furnished the political and administrative leaders of the Gorkhali Empire shifted their residence to Kathmandu after 1768, or the adjoining hill regions, but they owed their status to their origin in Gorkha, or the adjoining

---

6. Helmut Dan Schmidt and Wolfgang J. Mommsen, *"Imperialism", in Marxism, Communism and Western Society: A Comparative Encyclopaedia*, 1973, Vol. 4, p. 211.

regions, and to their caste and community, rather than to their new places of residence.

The narrow social and territorial base of the Gorkhali leadership precluded the allegiance of subject populations and territories outside the heartland to the Gorkhali *dhungo*, such as the *limbus* of the eastern hill region, the *tharus* and other communities of the Tarai, and the inhabitants of territories beyond the Bheri river, such as Jumla, Doti, Kumaun and Garhwal. They were subject populations in the sense that they were denied participation in the political, administrative or military leadership of the Gorkhali Empire.

In an apparent effort to win the allegiance of these subject populations, the Gorkhali state assumed the role of protector. It thus provided participation to the inhabitants of the heartland and protection to the subject populations. The Limbus of Pallokirat were offered the protection of the Gorkhali State in July, 1774:[7]

> We have conquered your country by dint of our valor ... The country now belongs to us. But you too belong to us. We undertake the protection of your kinsmen. We pardon your crimes and confirm the customs and traditions, rights and privileges of your country. In case we confiscate your lands, may our ancestral gods destroy our Kingdom.

The concept of protection of subject populations can be discerned in Kumaun also. After the Gorkhali conquest, many prominent people fled from Kumaun to escape the rigors of Gorkhali rule. The Gorkhalis appealed to them to come back, promising to protect them and restore their property.[8]

Such assurances of protection are significant in the

---

7. Mahesh C. Regmi, *Land Tenure and Taxation in Nepal*, 1978 (reprint of 1963-68, 4-Volume ed.), p. 626.

8. Royal Appeal to Bahadur Jung and others, Falgun Sudi 15, 1852 (February 1796), *RRC*, Vol. 5, pp. 313-14).

context of the legitimacy of Gorkhali rule in Kumaun. They show that the Gorkhalis emphasized such legitimacy only by invoking the rights of a conqueror. They, therefore, made an attempt to broaden the foundations of the legitimacy of their rule, particularly with their policies on culture and religion. These policies were aimed at enhancing the prestige and sanctity of the Gorkhali rule, and identifying it with the fundamental values and symbols of orthodox Hinduism. They may, therefore, be described as cultural imperialism. No information is available about whether the former rulers of Kumaun, who were no less Hindu than the Gorkhalis, had applied the caste sanctions and strictures prescribed in the Hindu scriptures, and, if so, how. Accordingly, it is not possible to determine whether the Gorkhali policies meant the introduction of a new element or were only a reiteration or endorsement of existing practices.

In any case, the Gorkhali assurances of protection of its subject populations against external threats did not prevent them from increasing the burden of taxation, exacting forced and unpaid labour services, and otherwise absorbing resources from the subject populations. To be sure, the inhabitants of the heartland territories were also subjected to similar burdens, but the Gorkhali elites were usually exempt. The subject populations of the territories lost their own elites after the Gorkhali conquest.

The Gorkhali attitude toward the subject populations is well illustrated by their belief that "the Limbus and Lepchas (of Pallokirat) cannot be trusted"[9] and that "the inhabitants of Majhkirat do not have a pure heart[10]. Their

9. Royal letter to Purnananda Upadhyaya, Ashadh sudi 7, 1850 (June 1793) *RRC*, Vol. 5, pp. 251-56; Regulations for Chainpur, Marga badi 3, 1869 (November 1812) *RRC*, Vol. 41, p. 181. According to this document, "Limbus, Lapches, and Bhotes cannot be trusted".

10. Royal letter to Subba Hemakarna Thapa, Bhadra sudi 1, 1864 (August 1807), *RRC*, Vol. 6, p. 1035.

attitude toward their subject populations in other parts of the Empire has not had similar documentation. One can only note that this distrust was fully reciprocated by the subject populations, who had little inclination to identify their interests with those of their Gorkhali masters. According to a recent British study, the Gorkhali forces which fought against the British during the 1814-16 war included "considerable numbers of western hillmen, including Garhwalis and Kumaunis, who, while loyal to their local commanders, were far from considering themselves citizens of Nepal, and cared little for far-off Kathmandu."[11] Indeed, the inhabitants of several territories conquered by Gorkha, particularly those in the regions east of the Dudhkosi river and west of the Bheri river, long remained unreconciled to Gorkhali suzerainty, and engaged in armed insurrections whenever the opportunity was favourable.

The Gorkhali administration in Kumaun has not attracted the attention of Nepali historians. Indeed, references to Kumaun are mostly limited to the year of its incorporation into the Gorkhali Empire, and the year of its cession to the British. Nothing has been written on how the Gorkhali rulers administered Kumaun, how they exploited its resources, and how the burden of defeat was borne by the people of Kumaun. The impact of Gorkhali rule in Kumaun on the Gorkhali state and society similarly remains unexplored. Some enterprising antiquarians have indeed brought into light a number of historical documents relating to Kumaun, but without any attempt at analysis and interpretation.

The Gorkhali record in Kumaun has long been a subject of controversy. Unfortunately, the controversy has been marked by nationalist prejudices. One Nepali historian has taken the stand that "the Gorkha administration presents a deep contrast to the succeeding British administration". He adds: "In spite of the alleged misrule, the Gorkhalis were

---

11. David Bolt, *Gurkhas*, 1967, p. 59.

commanding a great support from the general population (of Kumaun).[12] "On the other hand, according to a British source.[13]

> The success of the British (in Kumaun) was brought about more by the weakness of the enemy than by any skill and courage of their own .... The greatest source of weakness in the Gorkhali cause was the universal disaffection of the people of the country. Nothing could exceed the hatred which the tyranny and exaction of twenty-five years had created.

There seems little point in carrying ahead this conflict of opinion on the record of Gorkhali rule in Kumaun. An opinion is only as correct as the evidence that is produced in its support. Accordingly, I have tried in this volume to discuss the nature of Gorkhali rule in Kumaun on the basis of evidence that should be regarded as unimpeachable. I have presented my own stand on the controversy in the Epilogue. Scholars will then judge whether the evidence I have presented justifies my conclusions.

One thing is clear. The form and content of history are shaped as much by the perceptions of the historian as by the event of the past. As one writer has observed: "*The point of view of the historian enters irrevocably into every observation which he makes, history is shot through and through with relativity*". Indeed, "*even the categories in which experiences are subsumed, collected, and orders vary according to the social position of the observer*".[14] The historian's view of Gorkhali rule in Kumaun is thus shaped by his angle of vision. For a nationalist Gorkhali, the entire episode of the conquest and subjugation of the territory concerns the glory of the Gorkhali power, and its subsequent loss a result of British

---

12. D.R. Regmi, *Modern Nepal*, 1961, pp. 123-124.

13. Edwin T. Atkinson, *The Himalayan Districts of the North-Western Provinces of India*, 1882, Vol. 2, p. 654.

14. E.H. Carr, *What is History ?*, 1975, pp. 63-64.

imperialist designs. For one belonging to the erstwhile Gorkhali colonies, on the other hand, the reality is less abstract: " *The Gorkhali rule in Kumaun was a foreign rule.*"[15]

I have basically two aims in undertaking this effort. First, I want to establish a linkage between Nepali history and the experience of other societies in the world. For long Nepal's history has been treated as unique and unrelated to the world's experience. But the Gorkhali experiment in imperialism is certainly not a unique phenomenon in the history of the world, nor is the imperialist tendency to get rich through short cuts at the expense of weaker populations and territories a peculiar Gorkhali endowment. The story that I have tried to tell in this volume is thus only a familiar dish served with a Gorkhali sauce. Even within the Gorkhali Empire, the experience of Kumaun was by no means unique, for such other provinces as Doti and Garhwal also had more or less a similar experience. It has been rightly said that "what distinguishes the historian from the collector of historical facts is generalization."[16] That is to say, history is concerned with the unique only to arrive at generalizations which help in fitting with the broader human experience.

My aim is, therefore, "to bring Nepal into the mainstream of human thought".[17] I have put forward questions the answers to which may make it possible to compare experiences, and in addition, undertake studies of other societies within the same or a similar conceptual framework.

My second aim is more modest. It is to dig at the roots of the Nepali society of the present and promote an

15. Shiva Prasad Dabral, *Uttarakhanda Ka Rajanaitik Tatha Samskritik Itihas* (Political and cultural history of the Uttarakhanda region), 2030 (1973), pt. 5, p. 120.

16. Carr, p. 70.

17. Yadunath Khanal, *Nepal After Democratic Restoration*, 1996, p. 45.

understanding of the factors that have shaped its view of itself and of the world. Nationalism will have no meaning if the shared experience of the society is not analyzed and understood. Indeed, a collective amnesia of the past can hardly become the foundation of enlightened nationalism. A study of the Gorkhali imperial experience is thus of more than academic or antiquarian interest. It encompasses a formative period in the history of the modern Nepali state, and hence a proper understanding of that period is essential for a proper understanding of the modern state of Nepal as well.

The volume consists of seven Chapters in addition to the Prologue and the Epilogue. Chapter 1 describes the Gorkhali campaign of territorial expansion which ultimately transformed the Gorkhali state into an Empire. Chapter 2 deals with the logistic and other problems faced by the Gorkhalis in controlling and administering the distant province of Kumaun from their capital in Kathmandu. The next two chapters discuss the twin pillars of Gorkhali rule in Kumaun, namely, a provincial or regional administration (Chapter 3) and an army (Chapter 4). The revenue system is discussed in Chapter 5 and the *Jagir* system, under which the Gorkhali rulers paid emoluments to their officials and armymen, in Chapter 6. The final chapter contains an overview of the impact of the Gorkhali imperial rule on the people of Kumaun. The main findings and conclusions of the study are summarised in the Epilogue.

Mahesh C. Regmi

Contents

1

The Gorkhali Empire

Inclined to peace by his temper and situation, it was easy for him (Emperor Gaius Julius Ceasar Octavianus of Rome, 27 B.C.-14 A.D.) to discover that Rome, in her present exalted situation, had much less to hope than to fear from the chance of arms; and that, in the prosecution of remote wars, the undertaking becomes, every day more difficult, the event more doubtful, and the possession more precarious and less beneficial.

Edward Gibbon (1737-94)[1]

In 1786, if any one had told King Mohan Chand of Kumaun that the Gorkhali rulers, with their capital in Kathmandu, would conquer his Kingdom within five years, he would have been labelled as demented. The Gorkhalis had by that time extended their territories to the Kali-Gandaki river, but were still very far off from Almora, the capital of Kumaun. Between the two capitals were located more than twenty independent states along an 800-km stretch of the Himalayan region. King Mohan Chand would, therefore, have dismissed the probability of such an endeavor on the part of the Gorkhalis. Any lingering doubts that he might have had were assuaged by a treaty he signed in 1787 with Kathmandu, according to which "the friend of Gorkha is our friend, and the enemy of Gorkha is our enemy; both sides will work in the interests of each other."[2] But the unthinkable did happen. In early 1791, Gorkhali forces invaded Kumaun. Mohan Chand's son, Mahendra Chand, who was occupying the throne of Kumaun at that time, fled to the territories of the Nawab of Avadh. Kumaun then became one of the provinces of the Gorkhali Empire.[3]

Gorkha and Kumaun[4]

At the time when it embarked upon the campaign of territorial expansion during the 1740s, Gorkha was by no means an affluent or powerful state. It was deficient in resources and in opportunities of trade with Tibet as well as northern India. Gorkha then comprised approximately 970 square km in a triangular area east of Lamjung and Tanahu, with Tibet in the north and the Tanahu-held inner Tarai area of Chitwan in the south. Kumaun, in contrast, was a much bigger state in size and resources. It had a total area of about 8,000 square kilometers, located entirely in the Himalayan region, with Tibet in the north, the Tarai in the south, Garhwal in the west, and the Mahakali river in the east. The greater part of the province was situated in the mountainous zone.

There was also a marked contrast in the politics of these two states of the Himalayan region. The state of Gorkha, founded in 1559 by Drabya Shah, a prince of the ruling house of the adjoining state of Lamjung, enjoyed greater stability than the state of Kumaun. Its royal succession was strictly by primogeniture. Kumaun, on the other hand, had a monarchy, but no royal dynasty. Its political scene was marked by a series of usurpations, assassinations and incessant conflict between powerful factions, who, on more then one occasion, installed their puppets on the throne without any care for dynastic succession.

The Gorkhali state, however, had its own political problems. Despite dynastic stability, it suffered from prolonged political instability. Such instability owed its origin to the fact that during the 40 years between 1775, when Prithvi Narayan Shah died, and 1815, when the Gorkhali Empire crumbled as a result of a war with British India, the royal throne was occupied by minor Kings for a combined period of 32 years. The administration was actually run by various members of the royal family, including the Queen Mother (1778-85), the King's uncle (1785-94), a royal concubine (1800-3), the Chief Queen (1803-4), an ex-King who had abdicated the throne (1804-6), and even a member of the Gorkhali political leadership (1806-37), who was able to outwit or eliminate his political rivals. Lacking the legitimacy of the reigning King, they faced a constant threat to their position. Consequently, they needed a political base for themselves. Their attempts to secure such a base often conflicted with the interests and stability of the Gorkhali state. It is indeed significant that all the military campaigns of the Gorkhali Empire were launched during the periods when the throne was occupied by Kings who had not come of age. These campaigns included the conquest of the regions situated west of the Marsyangdi (1781-91), including Kumaun, the invasions of Tibet (July 1788-91), the Chinese attack (June - September 1792), the conquest of Garhwal and other areas up to the Sutlej river (1804-9), and the Gorkha-Britain war (1814-16). As such, they were influenced not only by military considerations, but by internal political considerations as well.

There was yet another important difference in the history of Kumaun and Gorkha. Kumaun warred incessantly with its neighbours on the east and the west, Doti and Garhwal, as well as with the Rohilla Muslims in the south. During 1743-44, for instance, the Rohillas invaded Kumaun and occupied Almora for about seven months. According to a British source, "They destroyed all the idols in the temples of Kumaun, and defiled them by the slaughter of cows, sprinkling the blood on the altars. Moreover, they melted down all the gold and silver idols and their ornaments. Gorkha too had occasional bickerings with its own hostile neighbours, particularly Kaski and Lamjung, but it never suffered from such external invasions and depredations.

The Expansion of Gorkha

The story begins in 1768-69, when King Prithvi Narayan

Shah of Gorkha conquered the three states of Kathmandu, Lalitpur, and Bhaktapur in Kathmandu valley. He then shifted the capital of the Gorkhali state from Gorkha to Kathmandu. In 1775, when he died, the Gorkhali state comprised the whole of the eastern Tarai, the eastern and central inner Tarai, the whole of Kathmandu valley, and the eastern hill region up to the Tista river bordering Sikkim, with the state of Jajarkot in the north-west as a vassal. Gorkha was well on its way to becoming an imperial power in the Himalayan region.

Prithvi Narayan Shah's son and successor, Pratap Simha, died in 1777 after a reign of less than three years. He was succeeded by his infant son, Ran Bahadur Shah. The campaign of conquest was then renewed by the Regent, the Dowager Queen Rajendra Laxmi (1777-85), and Bahadur Shah, Ran Bahadur's uncle (1785-94). Between 1781 and 1786, the Gorkhalis defeated the rulers of several states in the hill region west of Kathmandu, including Kaski, Lamjung, and Tanahu. By 1790, they had conquered the trans-Bheri states of Jumla, Dullu-Dailekh, Accham, Bajhang, Bajura, and Doti, extending the Gorkhali frontier to the Mahakali river.

By that time, the Gorkhalis had acquired a formidable reputation in the Himalayan region. The mere prospect of the Gorkhali advance struck terror in the minds of Gorkha's adversaries, and often made the conquest of their territories only a question of Gorkhali troops marching in. The Gorkhali victory over the state of Doti was thus achieved "without bloodshed" the ruler having fled before the Gorkhali advance.

In early 1791, the Gorkhalis crossed the Mahakali river, invaded Kumaun, and occupied the state within less then two months. The political situation in the region and the military capability of the Gorkhalis may have warranted such a step, but it was a clear breach of the 1787 treaty by the Gorkhali side.

Farther West

Wasting no time, the Gorkhalis then invaded Garhwal. The ruler, Pradyumna Shah, saw no alternative but to accept the status of vassal state within the Gorkhali Empire. Having invaded Tibet twice, in 1788 and 1791, the Gorkhalis realized the risk of fighting on two widely separated fronts simultaneously. They, therefore, agreed with that compromise, particularly since in 1792 the Chinese took retaliatory action and invaded the budding Empire. Fortunately, the wars with Tibet and China ended on terms which were neither humiliating nor catastrophic, and so had little permanent impact on the Gorkhali state and its military capability. Moreover, its imperialist acquisitions in the east, south, and west remained unaffected.

Under King Ran Bahadur

In 1794, Ran Bahadur Shah, who had already come of age, removed the Regent, Bahadur Shah, and took over the administration. The Gorkhali Empire at that time extended from the Tista river in the east to Kumaun in the west. It was comprised of at least eleven provinces outside the Gorkhali heartland: Chainpur, and Morang in the far-eastern region, Majhkirat, Saptari, Mahottari, Bara-Parsa Rautahat in the central region, and Jumla, Dullu-Dailekh, Doti, Accham, Pyuthan, and Kumaun in the region west of the Bheri river. It also included a number of vassal states. Jajarkot, Garhwal, Bajhang and Bajura in the Bheri-Mahakali region, and Mustang in the Dhaulagiri region. The hill state of Gorkha thus transformed itself into an Empire with a number of provinces and vassal states under its suzerainty.

The conquest of more than 50 states during a period of five years from 1786-1791 is clear evidence of imperialism. The Gorkhalis seem to have outpaced the British East India Company in the march toward the status of an imperial power. In the early 1790s, the British controlled the territories of Bengal and Bihar up to Benaras, with dependencies in Madras and Bombay. Such control could hardly be designated as imperialism. Indeed, a quarter-century would pass before one would speak of Britain's Indian Empire.[5]

During the five years of his rule (1794-99), Ran Bahadur followed an aggressive imperialist policy. That policy had three main dimensions. Firstly, several vassal states were annexed. Palpa and Salyan, although nominally independent, were treated as vassal states for all practical purposes. The other vassal states were given some measure of autonomy, but under strict Gorkhali control. The Gorkhalis stationed their troops in these vassal states, with the emoluments paid from the revenues of the states themselves. In other words, the people of those states were forced by the Gorkhali rulers to pay for their own subjugation and occupation themselves.[6]

The second aim of Ran Bahadur's imperial policy was to strengthen the capability of the Gorkhali army and its military installations. The army was expanded and reorganized and its salaries were standardized. Munitions production was stepped up. New forts were constructed in Kumaun, as well as in Dullu, Dailekh, Pyuthan, Doti, Bajura, Makwanpur, Chisapani, and other strategic areas.[7]

Finally, Ran Bahadur took a number of initiatives on the diplomatic front. He sent missions to the Sikh leaders of the Punjab states, including Patiala the Mughal Prince in Delhi and the King of Afghanistan in Kabul. Diplomatic missions were exchanged with the Marhatta military establishment in Delhi and Bhutan. A senior Gorkhali officer was sent to Lhasa with letters and gifts. Meanwhile, Ran Bahadur took steps to strengthen relations with the East India Company government in Calcutta.[8] Information is not available about the aims and achievements of these initiatives. One can only speculate that they were meant to project the new Empire's identity in the region. It is also possible that Kathmandu was trying to mobilize support for a campaign aimed at ousting the British presence in the sub-continent.

Ran Bahadur's preparations were completed by early 1799. The army was then mobilized with the intention of resuming the campaign of conquest in Garhwal and other areas west of Kumaun. New commanders were appointed in Gorkhali military units in areas situated west of the Marsyangdi river, including, Accham, Doti, Bajhang, and Bajura. They were then ordered to assemble their force in Kumaun.[9] A special officer was deputed to the region to inspect forts and other military installations and check whether or not Gorkhali military units were in full strength.[10]

However, a disaster struck the state of Gorkha which led to the postponement of these plans for almost six years. The main events which marked this turbulent period were King Ran Bahadur's taking a Brahmin girl as concubine (1797), her death, Ran Bahadur's abdication, installation of their infant son Girban Yuddha Bikram on the throne (1799), the emergence of a civil war situation between Ran Bahadur's faction and the faction which supported the infant King, and Ran Bahadur's four-year self-imposed exile in Benaras, India.

After 1804

The campaign of territorial expansion was taken up again when Ran Bahadur returned to Kathmandu in early 1804. In the meantime, profound changes had taken place in the military capability of the Gorkhalis. Indeed, the Gorkhali army which resumed the campaign of territorial expansion in the region west of Kumaun in 1804 was vastly different from the army which had conquered Kumaun in 1791.

There were two main causes of this change. The conquest of the Marsyangdi-Bheri region during 1781-86 added greatly to the military manpower of the Gorkhalis. The region possessed large populations of communities traditionally eligible for recruitment in the Gorkhali army, such as Khas, Magar and Gurung. This set it apart from other acquisitions such as the territories east of the Dudhkoshi river, inhabited by various ethnic groups such as Rai, Limbu and Sherpa, which were not so eligible. The region also possessed extensive mineral resources, particularly copper, which the Gorkhalis lost no time in exploited for the production of cannon and other weapons. By the early 1790s, the Gorkhali rulers were able to start a munitions industry of their own, possibly the only one in the Himalayan region. They produced almost all the weapons that they used in their campaign of territorial expansion: Cannon, muskets, swords and *khukuris*, and arrows. A munitions factory was started in Kathmandu in 1793 to manufacture cannon, muskets, and other weapons. Pyuthan was the location of another musket factory. The Gorkhalis also purchased muskets and other items from India to supplement the local production.[11]

Thanks to these initiatives, the Gorkhalis possessed the best equipment among the states of the Himalayan region. Such equipment, together with a standing army, made them the strongest power in the region. According to a recent British evaluation;, the Gorkhali Empire's:[12]

> .... great strength was the army by which it had been won and by which it was held, for no rival among the Himalayan states had a force more efficient and more loyal. Among the native princes of north India, only Ranjit Singh had a comparable army, but his energies and interests were centered more on Kashmir than on the Nepalese territories.

It was this rejuvenated Gorkhali state, self-confident of its growing military strength and bubbling with imperialist enthusiasm, that launched a new phase of expansion after Ran Bahadur's return from exile in March 1804. The state of Palpa was finally annexed, and the vassal state of Garhwal suffered the same fate a few months thereafter. Ambar Simha Thapa, a top-ranking Gorkhali leader, was given charge of the Gorkhali administration in the region west of the Marsyangdi river and designated supreme commander of the Gorkhali army on the western front. Under his command, the Gorkhalis conquered several states in the cis-Sutlej region and laid siege to the fort of Kangra, which has been described as "the most renowned stronghold in the Himalayas" [12]

The 1814-16 War and After

Meanwhile, another disaster struck the Gorkhali state's politics even while the Gorkhali imperial war games were being played on the western front. In February 1806, Ran Bahadur assumed the post of Regent under a royal order issued by his son, King Girban, who was then about six years old. The order granted him full powers in matters concerning administration, as well as war and peace. Three months later, he was assassinated by his half-brother, Sher Bahadur Shah. A bloody purge of the political leadership followed. In midst of the turmoil, Bhimsen Thapa, an obscure commander in Ran Bahadur's bodyguard during his exile in India, assumed the leadership of a new government.

The westward expansion of the Gorkhali state was not affected by these political troubles in Kathmandu. Military adventures continued in the cis-and trans-Sutlej region, culminating in the abortive four year siege of the Kangra fort. The tenacious campaign in Kangra is partly explained by the fact that for the Gorkhali rulers territorial acquisitions in the western Himalayan region were not an end in themselves, but only a stepping-stone toward further expansion, the ultimate goal being the conquest of Kashmir. The Kangra campaign marked the final phase of the Gorkhali campaign of territorial expansion. Plans to resume the attack of Kangra were checked by disputes with the East India Company, leading to the Gorkha-Britain war of 1814-16.

The imperialist ambitions of the Gorkhalis found expression in an initiative they took in mid-1814 for an alliance with the Marahatta and Sikh powers in India. The objective of that alliance was to oust the British power from the sub-continent and share it among themselves. The Gorkhali share was to comprise all territories west of the Tista river, as well as the plains north of the Ganges river, including the former territories of Kumaun. Significantly, the proposals placed Kashmir in the Sikh share. The proposals were leavened with an appeal to Hindu sentiment:

> Once the cavalry of the Sikhs and the Marahatta, and the infantry and muskets and cannon of the Gorkhalis, are joined together, God will make Hindus victorious in this war.

Envoys were sent to the Sikh ruler Ranjit Singh and the Marahatta rulers of Gwalior with these proposals, which were expected to be implemented within four or five years.[13]

Nothing is known about how the Indian rulers took those proposals, for they made no response at all. The Gorkhali authors of the proposal seem to have forgotten the fact that the Gorkhali Empire itself was founded on the debris of more than sixty independent Hindu states in the Himalayan region, often in contravention of bilateral non-aggression treaties. The appeal to Hindu sentiment would thus be regarded with distrust by the Sikhs and the Marahattas, or at least with a sense of bemusement. They must also have regarded the proposals with cynicism, for they were made on the eve of the Gorkhali war with the British.

Far from implementing these grandiose proposals, the Gorkhalis even lost the territories that they already controlled. Under a treaty they signed with the British at the end of the war in 1816, the Gorkhalis were forced to cede all territories beyond the Mechi river in the east and the Mahakali river in the west, including Kumaun. The territory of Kumaun thus remained a part of the Gorkhali Empire for about 25 years, from 1791 to 1815. About two months later, the East India Company restored a part of the ceded territories in the central and western Tarai regions. But the great days of Imperial Gorkha were over.

Anti-Gorkha Rebellions[14]

In the Prologue, I had mentioned that the inhabitants of several territories annexed by the Gorkhalis had engaged in armed rebellions against the Gorkhali state, particularly in the regions east of the Dudhkoshi and west of the Bheri.

Since these rebellions involved sections of the subject populations, the Gorkhali campaign of imperial expansion had a violent aspect which has paled into insignificance in Nepali historiography against the brilliance of the achievements.

The Rai inhabitants of the Dudhkoshi-Arun region were the first to organize a rebellion soon after the region came under Gorkhali control in 1773. During the war with China, the Murmis of Nuwakot, the Rais of Majhkirat, and the Limbus of Pallokirat again rose up in revolt. The Limbus even joined the Chinese side in large numbers to fight against the Gorkhalis. In the *trans*-Bheri region, the defeated states rebelled against the Gorkhali rule during the Chinese invasion. In Jumla, Sohan Shahi, a prince of the displaced ruling house who had taken refuge in Tibet after the Gorkhali conquest of that state, led the anti-Gorkhali rebellion with the active support of the local population. Similar insurrections were reported in Accham and Doti.

Within Kumaun itself, several areas in the Himalayan region long remained virtually outside Gorkhali control. In October 1795, King Ran Bahadur sent troops to those areas and brought them under Gorkhali control. The allegiance of the local people, however, remained doubtful. About seven years later, in July 1802, Kathmandu ordered the local administration to take military action and behead the ringleaders if the local inhabitants "hold up payments and assassinate tax collectors".

The Gorkhali penalty for rebellion was simple and ruthless. In 1792, one year after the conquest of Kumaun, Gorkhali authorities in that province were instructed to behead all rebels of above the age of 12 years. The Murmi and other rebels in the eastern hill region suffered the same fate in 1793. If rebels belonged to castes and communities which were traditionally exempt from the death penalty, they were degraded to a low caste, or punished with amputation of a limb, or skinned alive. The executions seem to have been carried out. For instance, in 1793 the Murmi rebels were told:

"We have received reports that you are still afraid of the death penalty. Have no fear; for those who were guilty have already been beheaded. A royal order of 1796 similarly told the Rais and Limbus that "those who had rebelled against (the Gorkhalis) at the time of the Chinese invasion have already been beheaded or otherwise punished."

Once the rebellions were suppressed, the Gorkhali chose the path of conciliation and proclaimed an amnesty. This happened as early as 1781 for the Rai rebels of Majhkirat. In 1796, King Ran Bahadur proclaimed a similar amnesty for the Rai and Limbu rebels. In early 1797, he granted a similar amnesty to Limbu, Bhote and other subject populations in the Arun-Tista region for any crime, including homicide, they might have committed during the rule of the defeated Sen Kings. In spite of this conciliatory step, sporadic incidents of rebellion took place among the Rais until 1808. In another conciliatory gesture, the royal family of Jumla, including the erstwhile ruler, Surabhan Shahi, his Queen, and the eldest prince, were allowed to reside in Pyuthan. In 1794, a royal order to the people of Jumla ruefully noted that "it has been five years since we occupied that territory, but you have all along caused us much trouble". It warned that if they again rebelled against Gorkhali rule, "Brahmins will be degraded to a low caste, and others will be punished with enslavement or death according to their caste status and the gravity of their crimes". In Accham, in contrast, the rebels prayed that they be punished with fines rather than with enslavement. The Gorkhalis accepted the plea and imposed fines. The rebellion was obviously not serious enough to warrant the death penalty. Indeed, the Gorkhalis seem to have taken the incident lightly, for 12 years later the fines had not been collected.

Sabotage and Subterfuge[15]

When overt acts of rebellion were not practicable, the subject populations often resorted to sabotage and subterfuge. These tactics were aimed at the tax policies of the Gorkhali rulers, and so cannot be regarded as a form of political protest. Even then they posed a challenge to the authority of the Gorkhali state. At Simta in Dailekh, for instance, the local landowners conspired to declare before a revenue settlement team from Kathmandu in 1808 that the territory had only tax-free temple lands, and no taxable lands whatsoever. One of the conspirators later changed his mind and so was murdered by his fellow-conspirators. The conspiracy was discovered only when his wife came to Kathmandu to file a complaint before the Gorkhali authorities. The assassin was sentenced to death, while the others were punished with amputation of their right hands.

Non-cultivation of taxable lands was another from of passive protest. The Limbus and Lepchas of the far-eastern hill region kept their taxable rice-fields barren while sowing crops on tax-free lands only, the obvious intention being to avoid taxation. They were, therefore, threatened with confiscation of their lands in addition to physical punishment if they continued their resistance.

Both of these incidents took place in territories situated outside the Gorkhali heartland. The official response to similar protests in the heartland was quite different. For instance, in 1805 the inhabitants of several villages in Kaski, to protest what they regarded as the high-handedness of armymen, (to whom rents from rice-fields tilled by them had been assigned as emoluments) stopped cultivating such lands and started bringing new hillside lands into cultivation. Instead of threatening the protestors with punishment, the Gorkhali rulers offered them various incentives. The contrast in official policy toward subject populations and the inhabitants of the Gorkhali heartland is striking.

Failure of Leadership

The success of the Gorkhalis in building an Empire that spanned the major part of the Himalayan region was a formidable display of the power of the Gorkhali war machine. It is no less a tribute to the Gorkhali political leadership, which had the vision and determination to turn the Gorkhali state into the first empire of that size in the Himalayan region. At the same time, one cannot avoid pointing out at least three cases in which the Gorkhali political leadership seems to have failed the test of statesmanship.

The most serious mistake of the Gorkhali political leadership was to make rapid advances on the western front after 1804. Indeed, it took the Gorkhali army less than one year to occupy the state of Garhwal and to begin the siege of the Kangra fort. Ultimately, the Gorkhalis faced a situation in which their military superiority was neutralized by the handicap of the ever-lengthening distance between the front and the center of decision-making authority in Kathmandu. The Kangra front, in fact, was more than 800 km from Kathmandu and presented formidable difficulties of transport and communications.

The logistical and other problems created by the distance between Kathmandu and the western front were compounded by yet another failure of the Gorkhali leadership. This was the failure to consolidate Gorkhali administrative control over the newly-conquered territories, including Kumaun and Garhwal. The Gorkhali authorities at the center had long realized the danger of overly rapid territorial advances. As early as January 1791, they had given a warning of the adverse consequences of proceeding ahead before bringing the conquered territories fully under Gorkhali control.[16] The commander of the Gorkhali forces on the western front, Kaji Ambar Simha Thapa, had also realized that danger, but too late. In a letter to the British General Ochterlony in December 1809, after Gorkhali forces had abandoned the siege of Kangra, Ambar Thapa admitted that "after an expense of crores of rupees and the loss of many men, I had for four years attacked that country and besieged the fort (of Kangra)." He also admitted that "leaving this country unsettled in my rear has caused all this trouble.[17]

The failure of the Gorkhali leadership to take advantage of a treaty the Gorkhali state had signed with the East India Company in 1801, when the ex-King Ran Bahadur Shah was living in self-exile in that country, must also be noted. The treaty established "a system of friendship" between the two sides. The articles of the treaty show that the British had no territorial claims on the Gorkhali State, and were willing to resolve" any dispute of boundary and territory through our respective vakeels or our officers, according to the principles of justice and right." It is a measure of the obtuseness of the Gorkhali political leadership that it was generally opposed to the treaty, accepting it only for fear lest the British should assist Ran Bahadur to regain his throne. In February 1804, the Governor-General, Lord Wellesley, reluctantly came to the conclusion that "the failure of the State of Nipaul in the fulfilment of its stipulations virtually constitutes the dissolution of the alliance," and therefore decided to abrogate the treaty. Rivalries within the political leadership thus deprived the Gorkhali state of a valuable opportunity to retain control over its territorial acquisitions. Thirteen years later, in December 1815, it was forced to sign the Sugauli treaty at the end of the Gorkha-Britain war, under which it lost even those territories that the British had recognized as Gorkhali possessions under the 1801 treaty.[18]

Concluding Remarks

In *Kings and Political Leaders of the Gorkhali Empire,* I put forward the view that the post-1804 Gorkhali campaign of imperial expansion was actually a series of barren and destructive adventure, devoid of any positive achievements. The Gorkhalis were unable to sustain any of their territorial gains in the western sector, and even lost the territory of Kumaun, which they had been occupying since 1791. There is no reason to reconsider that view. It may sound harsh, particularly in the light of the Gorkhali tradition of regarding the 1804-15 empire-building campaign as a glorious period in the history of the Gorkhali state, and revering the Gorkhali leaders of that campaign as national heroes. However, the search for truth necessarily makes the historian an iconoclast. He has to define the historical reality as he sees it, without permitting sentiment to influence his findings and conclusions. The reality is that the Gorkhali imperialist efforts after 1804 were nothing but a colossal waste of time, resources, and manpower, which caused immense hardships and sufferings to the people, and turned the Gorkhali Empire into a mere Kingdom.

NOTES

1. Edward Gibbon, *The Decline and Fall of the Roman Empire* (A one-volume abridgement by Dero A. Saunders), 1981, p. 28.

2. *Gorkha-Kumaun Sandhi* (The Gorkha-Kumaun treaty), Shaka Year 1709, corresponding to 1844, according to the Vikrama calendar, and 1787 according to the western calendar, in Yogi Naraharinath, *Sandhipatra Sangraha* (A collection of treaties and documents), 1966, p. 13.

3. The Gorkhalis occupied Almora on Chaitra 11, 1847 according to the Vikrama calendar (March 24, 1791). Mahesh Raj Pant, "*Nepal-Angrejale Yuddhako Ghoshana Nahundai Angrejle Gareko Yuddhako Tayari* " (War preparations of the English before the declaration of the Nepal-English War). *Purnima*, Vol. 2, No. 1, Baishakh 1, 2022 (April 13, 1965), p. 60.

4. The following account of political and other events is based on the following sources: Edwin T. Atkinson, *The Himalayan Districts of the North-Western Provinces of India*, 1882, Vol. 2, pp 582-606; and L. F. Stiller, *The Rise of the House of Gorkha*, 1975; and Leo E. Rose, *Nepal: Strategy for Survival*, 1971.

5. Percival Spear, *A History of India*, 1973, pp. 98 and 129.

6. The sources used in this paragraph are the following: Administrative regulations for Doti, Marga sudi, 1850 (November 1793). *RRC*, Vol. 36, pp. 37-40; separate royal orders to the *rajas* of Bajhang and Bajura to furnish troops to Sardar Bhakti Thapa, Shrawan sudi 10, 1851 (July 1794). *RRC*, Vol. 24, p. 313; Royal orders to the *rajas* of Gulmi, Palpa, Satahun, Bhirkot, Musikot, and Rising regarding

punishment to counterfeiters of coins, Shrawan sudi 11, 1851 (July 1794), *RRC*, Vol. 24, pp. 256, 309-10; separate orders to the *rajas* of Jajarkot, Bajhang, Bajura and Mustang to furnish toops for suppressing rebellion in Jumla, Bhadra sudi 11, 1851 (August 1794), *RRC*, Vol. 1A, p. 65. In 1796, the *raja* of Bhirkot, Shambhu Narayan Khan, was deposed and the territory was placed under the *subedar* of the Aridaman company, Kartik sudi 7, 1853 (October 1796), *RRC*, Vol. 23, p. 163; Ashadh badi 1854 (June 1797), *RRC*, Vol. 25, pp 495-96. Royal orders (1) to merchants of Palpa, Falgun sudi 9, 1853 (February 1797), *RRC*, Vol. 25, pp. 320-23; (2) regarding payments from Darma, Chaitra sudi 5, 1853 (March 1797), *RRC*, Vol. 25, p. 334; Separate orders to the *rajas* of Jajarkot, Bajhang, Bajura, Palpa, and Salyan to furnish troops for Kumaun, Chaitra sudi 2, 1800 (March 1804), *RRC*, Vol. 19, pp. 171-73. Instructions to Sardar Puran Shahi and others, Jestha badi 10, 1862 (May 1805), *RRC*, Vol. 20, pp. 209-15.

7. Separate royal orders to local authorities in Kumaun, Pyuthan, Doti, and other territories regarding construction of forts, Bhadra sudi 3, 12, and 13, 1853 (August 1796), *RRC*, Vol. 23, pp. 94-102; and Kartik badi 14, 1854 (October 1797), *RRC*, Vol. 25, p. 651.

8. Royal order to Subba Prabal Rana of Kumaun regarding gifts and presents to envoys of Daulat Singh of Delhi, Ashadh sudi 6, 1853 (June 1796), *RRC*, Vol. 23, pp. 78-79; separate orders to Subba Gaja Simha Khatri of Makwanpur, Chautariya Bam Shah, and Darogas Dayaram Padhya and Damodar Jaisi regarding gifts and presents to the Sikh leaders of Patiala, the Emperor of Kabul, and the Prince of Delhi, Chaitra sudi 15, 1854 (March 1798), *RRC*, Vól. 23, pp. 317-30; Royal orders to local functionaries from Kathmandu to Kumaun, Shrawan badi 10,1853 (July 1796), *RRC*, Vol. 23, p. 93; do. to envoy of Bhutan, Chaitra sudi 13, 1854 (March 1798), *RRC*, Vol. 23, p. 305; and to local functionaries between Kathmandu and Listi, Falgun sudi 13, 1855 (March 1799), *RRC*, Vol. 24, p. 716; Appointment of Dinanath Upadhyaya as Wakil in Calcutta, Aswin badi 14, 1853 (September 1796), *RRC*, Vol. 23, p. 78; Royal order regarding gifts of elephants to British officials in Calcutta,

Aswin sudi 14, 1853 (September 1796), *RRC*, Vol. 23, p. 57.

9. Royal orders to *subedars* in the trans-Marsyangdi region, Shrawan badi 3, 1855 (July 1798), *RRC*, Vol. 24, pp. 652-63.

10. Regulations for inspection of forts, bridges, etc. in the Marsyangdi-Kumaun region, Falgun badi 5, 1855 (March 1799), *RRC*, Vol. 24, pp. 703-9.

11. Mahesh C. Regmi, *Readings in Nepali Economic History*, 1979, pp. 36-45.

12. John Pemble, *The Invasion of Nepal*, p. 23.

13. Kaji Ambar Simha Thapa's instructions to Khardar Prithvivilas Upadhyaya for negotiations with the Sikhs, the Marahattas, and other powers in India on the formation of an anti-British alliance, Magh Badi 13, 1871 (January 1815); and report sent by Padmapani Sharma, Gorkhali envoy in Gwalior, Shrawan badi 1, 1871 (July 1814), in Chittaranjan Nepali, *Janaral Bhimasena Thapa ra Tatkalina Nepal* (General Bhimsen Thapa and contemporary Nepal), pp. 125-33 and 285-91.

14. This section is based on the following sources: Mahesh C. Regmi, *Kings and Political Leaders*, p. 17, n. 30; Mahesh C. Regmi, "The Royal Family of Jumla" *RRC*, Year 19, No. 1, January 1987, pp. 8-9, "Rebellion in Jumla," *Regmi Research Series*, Year 19, No. 5, May 1987, pp. 61-63; Mahesh Raj Pant, "Vir Bhakti Thapa," in *Purnima*, Year 3, No. 2, Shrawan 1, 2023 (July 16, 1966), p. 45, and *Purnima*, Year 3, No. 4, Magh 1, 2023 (January 14, 1967), pp. 55-57; Instructions to Subba Rudrabir Shah regarding administration of Kumaun, Shrawan badi 1, 1859 (July 1802), *RRC*, Vol. 24, pp. 579-85. Instruction to Subba Nar Shah regarding administration of Kumaun, Poush badi 2, 1849 (December 1792), *RRC*, Vol. 5, pp. 234-38; Royal order to Ajitan Shahi and others of Doti, Aswin badi 1, 1860 (September 1803), *RRC*, Vol. 19, pp. 125-26; Royal order to Hari Khadka reconfirming land grants in recognition of his help in quelling rebellion in Doti, Bhadra badi 11, 1873 (August 1816), *RRC*, Vol. 36, p. 309; Devi Prasad Bhandari (ed) , *Nepalako Samkshipta Itihasa*

(A Brief history of Nepal), *Purnima*, Year 16, No. 1, Falgun 2041 (March 1985), pp. 25-31.

15. Separate royal orders to different villages in Kaski, Shrawan badi 9, 1862 (July 1805), *RRC*, Vol. 6, pp. 229-31; to Gokul Padhya and others in Dhor, Jestha badi 4, 1862 (May 1805), *RRC*, Vol. 5, p. 521; to Limbus and other communities in Chainpur, Shrawan badi 9, 1862 (July 1805), *RRC*, Vol. 6, p. 222; and to *subedars* and *bicharis* in the trans-Bheri region, Falgun sudi 12, 1864 (March 1808), *RRC*, Vol. 13, p. 370.
16. *Purnima*, Year 3, No. 2, Shrawan 1, 2023 (July 16, 1966), p. 42.
17. Stiller, p. 239.
18. Regmi, *Kings and Political Leaders*, p. 45, n. 30.

2

Kathmandu and Almora

All these cities (in the Roman Empire, A.D. 98-180) were connected with each other and with the capital by the public highways. They united the subject of the most distant provinces by an easy and familiar intercourse, but their primary object had been to facilitate the marches of the legions; nor was any country considered as completely subdued till it had been rendered, in all its parts, pervious to the arms and authority of the conqueror. The advantage of receiving the earliest intelligence, and of conveying their orders with celerity, induced the emperors to establish throughout their extensive dominions the regular institution of post. House were everywhere erected at the distance only of five or six miles; each of them was constantly provided with forty horses; and by the help of these relays it was easy to travel an hundred miles in a day along the Roman roads.

Edward Gibbon[1] (1737-94)

As mentioned in the Prologue, one of the questions raised in this study is how the instruments of imperial control in the territories of the Gorkhali Empire worked in actual practice. Before discussing those instruments and their working, it is necessary to study the logistics, that is "the branch of military science having to do with procuring, maintaining, and transporting material, personnel, and facilities.[2] These logistics became even more critical after the annexation of Garhwal in 1804. Kumaun no longer remained a frontier province, but was used as a springboard for expansion toward the west. It lay on the route through which Gorkhali officials and troops travelled on their way to the western front and back. It was the conduit used by the Gorkhalis to supply men and material to the western front. This resulted in a tremendous increase in the volume of traffic through Kumaun. These needs could only be met by setting up a complex system of tracks, river crossings and supply of manpower. This chapter describes these systems.

The East-West Track

To cover the 800 km from Kathmandu to Almora required the crossing of inhospitable, rugged Himalayan mountain passes and countless rivers flowing from north to south. The Gorkhali rulers laid a rough track between the two places, extending it gradually toward the west as the frontiers of the Empire expanded. The track connected Pokhara, Pyuthan, Salyan, Dailekh, Accham, Doti, Kumaun, and Garhwal, and then to the western front.[3] Because of the terrain, the track, in the words of a twentieth-century British observer, was obstructed by many steep ascents and descents, and was practically impassable during flood-time. The entire length of the route "runs through the under-features of the Himalayas, under-features which in any other country would be hailed as mountains of importance, and the pace is necessarily slow." Indeed, travel through the east-west track between Kathmandu and Almora consisted of "little else than a perpetual climb, a perpetual descent, and a perpetual river crossing.[4] Only after the introduction of railroad facilities during the closing years of the 19th century[5] did east-west travel within Nepal through the plains of northern India become a practical alternative.

River Crossing Facilities

It was the crossing of rivers that made travel along the east-west track particularly arduous and risky. The major rivers on the route included the Trishuli, the Marsyangdi, the Seti, the Kali-Gandaki, the Bheri, the Karnali, and the Mahakali. Crossing-points on such rivers were known as *ghat*, that is, a landing place.[6] There were at least 32 *ghats* in the western hill regions up to the Kali-Gandaki river. The number of *ghats* on the Bheri, Karnali, and Mahakali rivers, and their locations are not known.[6]

There were two main ways of crossing rivers at the *ghats*: *sanghu* and *targhat* or *jhula*. *Sanghus* were logs placed across shallow points on rivers and streams, elaborated in the western Himalayan region with a more complex design:[7] Successive layers of timber, laid from either bank, gradually project like an arch, and reduce the interval to such an extent as to admit a single plan. This is usually 2 or 3 feet in width.

The *targhat* or *jhula* was built across wider streams: Ordinarily it meant "bridges of ropes made of rattans connected by cords of rough grass.[8] Another British source mentions the "efficient, but sometimes terrifying *jholunga*, a suspension bridge of bamboo and creeper" which had to be replaced after each monsoon.[9] In the western Himalayan region, their design has been described as follows:[10]

> Two parallel rope cables are stretched across the streams, and from these in suspended a ladder-like roadway, consisting of small flat pieces of wood, lashed a full step apart. The two cables form a sort of balustrade, and the lengths of rope (nearly a yard in length) which tie the small planks (from 1 to 2 feet in length) act as palings. In order that the cables may not break under the strain, travellers cross the jhula bridge one by one.

The river-crossing facilities mentioned above were operated by men belonging to the *majhi* community, who traditionally worked as fishermen or ferrymen. There were *majhi* settlements near *ghats* on most of the big rivers. The headman of each such settlement, who was known as *mijhar*, managed the facilites. His main duty was to transport troops and military supplies across the river "without a moment's delay." After 1804, many *majhis* in the western region were sent to the western front to cope with the increased volume of traffic.[11]

Transport and communications between Kathmandu and Kumaun, never quick and swift in the best of times, were further disrupted every year during the monsoon season, July through September. The major rivers were flooded during those months, and even tiny rivulets and dry ravines became surging torrents. Tracks that had been cleared earlier were washed away and so needed fresh repairs every year. *Sanghus* were generally out of operation during the monsoon, but *targhats* continued to be used for the movement of both men and military equipment.[12]

It was by no means an easy task for the Gorkhali officers and armymen to travel along the track between Kathmandu and Kumaun and from there to the western front at Kangra beyond the Sutlej river. According to a British source, in 1814.[13]

> On the banks of the Ganges and within our territory there is a point in the route of communication between the seat of Government at Nipaul and their possessions to the westward by which the reinforcements proceeding to the (Gorkhali) army and travellers of every description are obliged to pass. After descending a high hill to the eastward, the road leads across a plain to the left bank of the Ganges. This plain is in the possession of the British Government. The river being unfordable, a boat is maintained by the Nipaulese on the opposite side which is in their territory; it used until lately to be kept on the eastern side. Scarcely a day passes that some soldiers do not go or return by this route. They are seldom in parties exceding 20 or 30 (for in the present desolate condition of the country a greater number cannot find subsistence on the march).

It was in this way that the Gorkhalis built up, expanded, and ultimately lost the Empire. It is, therefore, hardly surprising that Gorkhali officials and armymen were given as many as seven months to join their duties in Kumaun. In 1804, when the campaign of territorial expansion was revived, the period was shortened to 50 days.[14]

Mode of Travel

Top-ranking Gorkhalis were carried between Kathmandu and Almora and other destinations in palanquins, whereas those belonging to the lower ranks travelled on foot.[15] Colonel William Kirkpatrick, a British officer who visited Nuwakot and Kathmandu for about four weeks in early 1793, described the Gorkhali palanquin as follows:[16]

> Travellers are very often conveyed over the mountains in Dhokas, which are usually made of bamboos, somewhat of the form of an inverted truncated cone. The carriages employ instead of Palanwuins a sort of hammock. They consist of Durwar, or cotton, sack, slung upon a pole. From four to eight bearers are assigned to each, two or four (according to the weight of the person in it) being under the pole together. When four are necessary, they usually fix a stick horizontally across each extemity of the main pole, one man supporting each end of the two cross sticks.

The central authorities made special travel arrangements for foreign envoys and other important people. For instance, in June 1805, an envoy from Kangra visited Kathmandu for talks with the Gorkhali authorities. For his return, Gorkhali officials and armymen in Pyuthan, Accham, Doti and Kumaun were ordered to provide an escort of four armymen each up to Garhwal. They were also ordered to arrange for his accommodation, food, and porters and bearers at each halting place, and to take special care of him while crossing rivers.[17]

Travel Restrictions and Impediments

This account of the elaborate infrastructure built by the Gorkhali rulers for transport and communications between Kathmandu and Almora should not give the impression that anybody was free to travel within the Gorkhali Empire or to inter Kathmandu. This was by no means the case. The Gorkhali rulers imposed access restrictions on people visiting Kathmandu from the provinces, and even from other areas in the Gorkhali heartland. Such restrictions were meant to keep out "undesirable people such as medicants, beggars, destitute people, jugglers, and actors".[18]

The policy of isolating Kathmandu from other territories of the Gorkhali Empire was achieved with two sets of measures. Firstly, the Gorkhali rulers introduced a passport system for visiting or leaving Kathmandu. Such passports needed the signatures of top-ranking authorities, both in Kathmandu and on the western front.[19] These restrictions outlived the Gorkhali Empire and remained intact in more or less the same form during the Rana period (1846-1951) and beyond.[20] Secondly, the Gorkhali rulers kept only a few routes open between Kathmandu and other parts of the Empire, closing all unauthorized tracks by making them unusable. Local functionaries in areas adjoining Kathmandu on all sides were ordered to find out if any one had opened unauthorized tracks to close such tracks with snares and thorny bushes, and to arrest any one who travelled through such tracks, or, if he attempted to evade arrest, shoot at him with poison-tipped arrows. People who tilled these prohibited tracks for cultivation of crops were punished with death, confiscation of property, or banishment.[21]

As mentioned above, only a few routes were kept open between Kathmandu and the south. One of those routes passed through Chisapani in the modern Makwanpur district, the site of an important fort, with the adjoining village containing "about twenty thatched houses". The Chisapani route was a formidable one because of the terrain as well as official restrictions. According to Kirkpatrick, who travelled through that route in 1793, "the road traverses the side of the mountain and in many places lies close to the brink of frightful precipices," He adds:

> The ascent (to Chisapani from the south) is in many places very steep; besides which the footing is rendered not a litle insecure by the loose fragments of rock which are scattered through it."[22]

In 1799, a landowner of Makwanpur was given the responsibility of closing an unauthorized track through Bhichhakhori, a village south of Chisapani.[23]

The wisdom of the strict ban on the use of unauthorized tracks was seen during the last days of the Gorkha-Britain war. In February 1816, the British General Ochterlony led a force of about 20,000 fighting men through Makwanpur, which was "the last major defense of Kathmandu".[24] According to a British source, Ochterlony outflanked a well-fortified defensive system in the hills, by making a daring night march up a little-used goat track which had been overlooked.[25]

Administrative restrictions and geographical constraints were not the sole factors keeping Kathmandu in a state of virtual isolation. Malaria was another major hurdle. According to a recent British study, "because of the malaria, merely to walk in the Tarai during the hot and rainy seasons was death".[25] In 1876, the British Resident in Kathmandu reported to his government: The fear of malaria amongst Gorkhalis ... ... is so great that they would rather have their heads cut off than submit to it".[26] The following royal order issued to local authorities on the route between Kathmandu and the southern plains through Chisapani in April 1806 illustrates the nature of the problem:[27]

> The royal priest is visting Kathmandu for a few days from Calcutta. This is the malarial season. He may fall ill if he stays at a malarial place twice, while coming here and returning to Calcutta, thereby hampering our work. Accordingly, you are ordered to send your armymen and arrange for relays of porters and bearers, so as to make it possible for him to halt at a place in the hill, instead of at a malarial place. Make arrangements to ensure that as soon as he enters our territory from Patna he is taken quickly to Chisapani.

Labour Services

The previous sections have discussed the logistical problems for transport and communications which the Gorkhali faced between Kathmandu and Kumaun. This discussion underlines one crucial aspect of the Gorkhali imperial system, namely, the need to harness manpower on a growing scale. The purposes were varied. They included the regular repair and maintenance of the east-west track, which seldom survived the next monsoon, and porterage services for the of men, material, and official mail. The terrain made the use of pack animals impractical. Everything had to be carried through the east-west track on the human back[28] in addition, labour services were needed to construct and repair tracks, forts, bridges, and irrigation canals, to bring waste lands under cultivation, and to supply materials such as firewood, or charcoal, needed by civil and military establishments.[24] This extensive use of labour services virtually turned the Gorkhali Empire into a vast labour camp.

How did the Gorkhalis meet this massive demand for labour ? The question is important, since they lacked the resources needed for payment of wages. The answer is simple. The Gorkhali rulers solved the problem in the same way imperialist rulers have done so everywhere in the world throughout history. They forced the inhabitants of the occupied areas to provide labour services without wages. A few examples from the experience of some other states through the centuries may be illuminating. In the Roman Empire, the state "demanded labor from the people of the provinces for the construction of roads, military transport and other public workds"[30] In medieval Europe, most of the population was "subject to legally defined forced labour, for example, road work, transport services and other feudal obligations.[31] During the early years of the 18th century, the English fleet was maintained through the press gang, that is, "a group of men who round up other men and force them into naval or military service",[32] voluntary recruitment being inadequate.[33]

The Gorkhali rule in the western Himalayan region was by no means an exception to this universal rule. Both the

Gorkhali state and the state of Kumaun met their labour needs through the system of forced and unpaid labour. It is indeed significant that in Kumaun this system remained in force even after the Gorkhalis ceded it to the British in 1815. The reasons why the British had no alternative but to do so sheds light on the raison d'etre of the system. According to a recent study:[34]

> The British operated the system, a legacy of the petty hill chiefs who preceded them, on grounds of administrative convenience in tracts whose physical situation made both commerical transport and boarding houses economically unattractive... While convinced of the "inequity of the practice" as early as 1850, the (British) government concluded after an enquiry that there existed no available substitute.

Nor was this situation confined to Kumaun. An official British report on the availability of porters in the territory of Garhwal, published in 1896, states:[35]

> Owing to the contracted state of the population, the insufferable indolence of the male part of it, their general aversion to carrying burthens, the nature of every species of labour in this province, whether on public works or in transport, has always been compulsory.

The problem thus had two dimensions: A general scarcity of manpower and lack of money to pay wages. The forced labour system met both these needs simultaneously. Indeed, forced labour services were the grease that lubricated the wheels of the Gorkhali Empire.

Two terms were used in the Gorkhali Empire to denote the forced labour system-*jhara* and *begar*. *Jhara*, apparently a term of indigenous origin, was used in the hill and mountain regions, and *begar*, of Persian origin, in the Tarai regions. In order to avoid confusion, I shall use the term *jhara* for forced labor services exacted by the state, and *begar* for similar services exacted in an unauthorized manner by Gorkhali officials and armymen for their own needs. The *jhara* system in this sense will be described in this chapter, and the *begar* system in Chapter 7.

In the present context, the most important aspect of the *jhara* system is its use for transport and communications between Kathmandu and Almora and the western front. Indeed, the system was used on a massive scale for the transportation of such important materials as arms and ammunition and official mail.

The following example illustrates how the *jhara* system worked for the transportation of arms and ammunition from Kathmandu to Kumaun and other destinations on the western front. In September, 1809, Kaji Nayan Simha Thapa, a brother of Bhimsen Thapa, was sent to the Kangra front. A consignment of cannon and other weapons and ammunition was despatched along with his party. It was instructed to send soldiers to round up *jhara* porters one or two days, before hand, so that the consignment might not be held up anywhere. *Majhis* at crossing points on the rivers were ordered to join the party at the rate of one man from each seven households. Local functionaries were ordered to round up *majhis* and porters on *jhara* basis and arrange for the expeditious despatch of the consignment.[35] An official advance team had been deputed to inspect river-crossing facilities between Kathmandu and Kumaun and to take action against the local authorities wherever the consignments were held up.[36] A royal order to local authorities in the Marsyangdi-Kumaun region stated:[37]

> Cannon and other weapons and ammunition are being despatched in large quantities to the western front. The existing facilities have become inadequate. You are, therefore, ordered to send soldiers to round up *jhara* porters from villages situated within a redius of one or two days journey toward both the north and the south, so that the weapons are transported day and night without a moment's delay up to Pyuthan.

From Pyuthan, the consignment was escorted by five armymen up to Achham. From Achham, a similar escort was provided up to Doti and then to Kumaun and Srinagar in Garhwal in the same manner.[38] More places were added to the list as the Gorkhalis extended their territorial conquests further westward.[39]

Thanks to these arrangements, the Gorkhalis were able to maintain a regular flow of arms and ammunition between Kathmandu and the western front. The scale of the flow may be imagined from the fact that in January 1806, a single consignment of arms and ammunition sent from Kathmandu to the front was comprised of 500 cannon-balls, 24,000 shots, and 4,000 flints, in addition to large quantities of steel and gunpowder.[40]

The Hulak System

As noted previously, the *jhara* system was used for the transportation of official mail and military supplies from Kathmandu to Almora and other destinations. *Jhara* services for such purposes were of a special kind, for it was not practicable to impress the same porters throughout the entire route. It was difficult to demand porters to carry loads to places located at a long distance from their villages and then return home by the same route. Such a practice would also undermine the speed of despatch, for the continuous work of carrying for several days in succession without a rest was exhausting and therefore slow. The Gorkhali rulers made an attempt to solve these problems by setting up relays of *jhara* porters from one point to another along the east-west track. Thus porters carried loads only for about two or three hours a day. The relay system was known as *hulak*.

Arrangements for the transportation of government supplies by relays of porters under the *hulak* system were made for specific purposes in different parts of the Empire on an *ad hoc* basis whenever necessary. The relays were organized by impressing porters from among the available men at each point. But these points were specified neither by the central nor by the provincial authorities. The latter were ordered to arrange for relays only up to places under their jurisdiction where the number of households was at least four. They were often instructed to send troops to organize the relays two days in advance. Despite all these efforts, delays were inevitable. The following warning issued in June 1806 to the local authorities from Kathmandu to Kumaun, shows this clearly:[41]

> We have already warned you two or three times that you shall be punished if you make even a single moment's delay in transporting arms and ammunition to Kumaun. If you again disobey that order and hold up such supplies at any point, you may be punished with confiscation of property and enslavement.

The break down of the *ad hoc* use of *hulak* services for the transportation of official supplies over long distances ultimately led to the creation of a formal institutional organization, marking the final stage in the development of the *hulak* system. A two-way *hulak* line for official mail between Kathmandu and Kumaun was established for the first time in April 1804, coinciding with plans to conquer territories in the region west of Kumaun, including Garhwal. Permanent *hulak* posts were set up at intervals of approximately 3 km, with eight mail-carriers at each post round the clock. They were warned that they would be punished if they defaulted, but no incentive was provided beyond exemption from *jhara* obligations for other purposes.[42] This did not provide any actual benefit to the *hulak* mail-carriers, since the same person cannot be employed for two different purposes simultaneously.

These onerous arrangements did not satisfy the mail-carriers. Consequently, they abandoned their posts in numbers large enough to merit an official inquiry in early 1807. At least three weaknesses were identified: The inadequate number of *hulak* households at some places, the long distance that each relay had to cover, and inadequate incentives. Accordingly, an official team was sent to areas west of Kathmandu in early 1807 with orders to enroll the necessary number of households and also to relocate *hulak* posts wherever necessary. Its other duties were as follows:[43]

> In case the location of hulak posts at intervals of one day's journey is too distant, relocate them at intervals of 2 or 3 hours journey. Enroll 16 households at easy places, and 24 households at difficult places. Keep 6 men in readiness all the 24 hours of the day; so that they may run to the next hulak post without a moment's delay as soon as mail is received, day or night, morning or evening.

Within Kumaun itself, at least 54 *hulak* posts were set up in July 1807 manned by 891 households.[44]

Finally, the 1807 arrangements increased incentives to *hulak* mail-carriers. In addition to exemption from forced labour for other purposes, they were given a 50 percent rebate in homestead taxes, and security of tenure on their homesteads and rice-fields, on the condition that they paid the rents due on such lands.

The *hulak* arrangements for the transportation of official mail in 1804 and 1807, as described above, did not cover arms, ammunition, and other government supplies. Accordingly, these supplies continued to be transported on the basis of *ad hoc* arrangements. Two years later, in June 1809, permanent *hulak* arrangements were made for the transportation of government supplies as well, but only for the Kathmandu-Bheri region. Between two and four *hulak* posts were established according to the nature of the terrain at intervals of one day's journey, with 20 households for each post.[45] The 1809 reforms also provided more benefits to *hulak* porters of both categories in the Kathmandu-Bheri region. Taxes on the homestead were fully waived, while other taxes were remitted at the rate of one rupee per household. Tenancy rights on rice-lands tilled by *hulak* porters were guaranteed. Rice-land allotments between 40 *muris* and 100 *muris* (0.5 to 1.25 hectare) according to the size of the family were also promised. West of the Bheri river, government supplies continued to be transported through *ad hoc hulak* relays. The *hulak* lines of both categories were reorganized under eight regional headquarters, located in Pokhara, Pyuthan, Salyan, Achham, Dipayal, Almora, Srinagar and Doon.[46]

The central authorities took special care to ensure that the east-west track and river-crossing and *hulak* facilities remained in continuous operation through regular repairs and maintenance. Almost every year, they deputed special teams to inspect such facilities.[47]

Declining Supplies

This brief outline of the *hulak* system introduced by the Gorkhali rulers between Kathmandu and Almora during the period 1804 through 1809 raises a number of questions. Why were permanent *hulak* posts established in 1804 only for official mail and not for arms and ammunition and other government supplies ? Why were such posts for supplies established in 1809 for the Kathmandu-Bheri region only ? In the absence of any clues in official sources, I can only put forward what I consider logical explanations.

The main point is that of bulk. A single mail-bag can contain hundreds of official documents, easily carried by a porter over a distance of two or three hours' journey from one *hulak* post to another. Accordingly, a *hulak* post for official mail could be adequately staffed by only six porters kept ready round the clock. In contrast, arms and ammunition and other official supplies were bulky in weight and large in quantity. The total weight of these supplies, the number of *hulak* porters needed to carry them and the frequency of despatch cannot be ascertained, but there can be no doubt that permanent *hulak* posts with only six or even ten porters each could not handle such large consignments. Even if it was possible to raise the strength of the *hulak* posts, consignments could not be despatched every day, so the men would have to remain idle most of the time. In other words, arrangements for permanent *hulak* posts were not flexible enough for the transportation of large-scale but intermittent consignments of bulky military supplies.

There is one flaw in this line of reasoning. The constraints that I have mentioned above were applicable in 1809 as well. Nevertheless, it was in that year that permanent *hulak* posts were established in the Kathmandu-Bheri region for government supplies. Why were the constraints which the Gorkhali rulers faced in 1804 not valid five years later ? The answers to these questions lie on an important event that happened in the course of. the Gorkhali campaign beyond the Sutlej river. As noted in Chapter 1 (The Gorkhali Empire). The Gorkhalis had laid siege to the fort of Kangra in late 1805. In April 1809, the Sikh leader Ranjit Singh signed a treaty with the British, establishing his rights to the territories situated west of the Sutlej river. The treaty thus made the Gorkhaki presence in the Kangra region untenable. The Sikhs lost no time in marching toward the fort, and actually occupied it within a few months. Clashes then started between the Gorkhali and Sikh armies. The Gorkhalis had no alternative but to lift the siege of the Kangra fort and even vacate the areas west of the Sutlej river. The prolonged siege was the main reason for the supply of arms and ammunition from Kathmandu and Pyuthan on a large scale, the withdrawal naturally made large-scale supplies unnecessary. It was against this backdrop that Kathmandu established the Kathmandu-Bheri *hulak* line for the transportation of arms and ammunition, and other supplies. The central authorities may have backed the siege of the Kangra fort, but apparently did not approve of the clashes with the Sikhs and other military adventures in the region between the Sutlej and Jamuna rivers. This may have been one of the reason why they did not furnish the reinforcements requested by the Gorkhali authorities on the western front. In June 1809 they limited the flow of supplies to a level which could be handled by a *hulak* force of 20 households against 16 to 24 households for the *hulak* mail service.

Working of the Hulak System

Notwithstanding these elaborate arrangements, *hulak* services of both categories were marked by delays and obstructions. It took several weeks for official mail to reach Kathmandu from Almora and other destinations in the west. For instance, in 1806 an official report from the Kangra front reached Kathmandu in 34 days.[48] About eight years later, in 1815, a similar report from Srinagar in Garhwal reached Kathmandu in as many as 50 days.[49] The reasons for delay, however, depend as much on physical conditions as on administrative shortcomings. About four decades, later, in 1854, the Rana Prime Minister Jung Bahadur promulgated a law prescribing the time for travel between Kathmandu and the outlying territories. That law allowed a period of 30 days for a mail-carrier to travel from Kathmandu to Doti.[50] But even if one week is allowed for travelling from Doti to Almora a one-way trip between Kathmandu and Almora would take about 37 days. The record set by the Gorkhali rulers thus remained unbroken for several subsequent decades.

The situation was even worse for *hulak* services for the transport of government supplies. Delays were frequent, as shown by official orders to the local authorities to speed up despatches. There were also occasional cases of sabotage and negligence, but the Gorkhali response was invariably swift and severe. In one such incident in October 1805, one piece of cannon despatched from Kathmandu was found to have been held up in Salyan for three days. It was later found hidden in a hay stack at some distance from the main track. The local authorities were ordered to arrest the guilty men and send them to Kathmandu in irons.[51]

The high-handed methods used by the Gorkhali authorities in the mobilization of *hulak* services, created more problems. According to a royal order of 1808, for instance, soldiers who had been deputed to organize *hulak* services on the east-west track were told.[52]

> we have received reports that at places where the number of *hulak* households is small and not enough of porters are available, you seize the sons and daughters of the people, beat them, and force them to carry loads even when they offer to increase the number of relays. (In the future), increase the number of relays for the transportation of government supplies and arms and ammunition in villages where (the number of *hulaki* households) is small. Any persons who beats the wives, sons, and daughters of the people for transporting his own suppiies, other than those of the government, will be punished.

The ban on the use of *hulak* services for personal purposes was repeated in October 1810, for the region west of Kathmandu up to the Jamuna river.[53]

> You are hereby ordered to provide hulak services only for arms and ammunitions, and sick or injured persons. Do not provide such services to Gorkhali officials or other for their personal purposes. In case any one compels you to do so, demand wages at the rate of 2 *annas* a day. If he does not agree to pay, submit a complaint to us. The local authorities shall keep porters ready to work on wages whenever troops travel through the areas under their jurisdiction.

It is significant that the central authorities issued an almost identical order about four decades later in 1849, when the Rana Jung Bahadur was Prime Minister.[54]

In any case, such repeated appeals and exhortations made not the slightest dent on the problem. In November 1814, when the Gorkha-British war began, the Gorkhali rulers made a last-minute attempt to eliminate delays and obstructions in *hulak* services between Kathmandu and the western front. A three-member official team was appointed for this purpose.[55] It is difficult to believe that the team was able to start its work or even to visit the region under its jurisdiction at a time when fighting had already started.

Concluding Remarks

The defects of the systems introduced by the Gorkhali rulers for transport and communications between Kathmandu and Almora and other destinations on the western front should not blind us to the success they achieved in retaining their imperial control over Kumaun for a quarter-century and fighting a war with the British in which they initially had the upper hand. The reasons for their ultimate defeat are many and complex, but it cannot be denied that men and material did reach the front from Kathmandu and other parts of the Empire. What went wrong was actually due to some basic weaknesses of the Gorkhali imperial system, the most important of which were its inability to win the cooperation of the subject populations and its coercive methods for mobilizing forced labour services. The peasants of the Gorkhali Empire obviously did not share the enthusiasm of their masters in stepping up the imperial war efforts.

The *hulak* services introduced by the leaders of the Gorkhali Empire outlived the imperial period. The mail services were abolished in 1913 and services for the transport of government supplies a few years after the end of Rana rule.[56] This may be regarded as evidence that there were no alternatives to the *hulak* system. The Gorkhali Empire may have used coercive methods in exacting forced labour services from their subjects, but their realistic approach to the problem of transport and communications between Kathmandu and the outlying territories of the Empire must certainly be understood, if not admired. To be sure, the burden of these services fell on the people whereas the glory of success and the ignominy of defeat belonged to the Gorkhali leaders. But in history "those who pay the cost are rarely those who reap the benefits".[57]

NOTES

1. Edward Gibbon, *The Decline and Fall of the Roman Empire*, (A one-volume abridgement by Dero A. Saunders), 1981, pp. 74-75.

2. David B. Guralnik (ed.), *Webster's New World Dictionary*, 1972, p. 832.

3. Arrangements for transportation of arms and ammunition from Kathmandu to Srinagar, Bhadra badi 3, 1864 (August 1807), *RRC*, Vol. 20, p. 377.

4. Percival Landon, *Nepal* (1978 reprint of 1928 ed.), 1978, Vol. 2, p. 41).

5. Mahesh C. Regmi, *An Economic History of Nepal, 1846-1901*, 1988, pp. 207-9.

6. H.H Wilson, , *A Glossary of Revenue and Judicial Terms and Useful words Occurring in Official Documents Relating to the Administration of British India* (reprint of 1855 ed.), 1978, p. 175.

7. S.D. Pant, *The Social Economy of the Himalayans*, 1935, p. 203.

8. Francis Hamilton, *An Account of the Kingdom of Nepal*, 1971 (reprint of 1819 ed.), p. 274.

9. (British) Ministry of Defense, *Nepal and the Gurkhas*, 1965, p. 13.

10. Pant, p. 203.

11. Dor Bahadur Bista, *People of Nepal*, 1967, p. 118; Royal order to *majhis* and *mijhars* at different *ghats* on the Trishuli, Marsyangdi, Karnali, and other rivers, Aswin badi 12, 1862 (September 1805), *RRC*, Vol. 6, pp. 472-75; Baishakh sudi 1, 1864 (April 1807), *RRC*, Vol. 6, pp. 876-77 and 895-99; Marga sudi 1, 1849 (November 1792), *RRC*, Vol. 25. p. 282; and Aswin badi 6, 1864 (September 1807), *RRC*, Vol. 40, p. 101.

12. Royal orders to local authorities in Pyuthan, Achham, Doti, and Kumaun, and the *majhis* of *ghats* between the Bishnumati river in Kathmandu and Srinagar in Garhwal, Aswin badi 2, 1862 (September 1805), *RRC*, Vol. 6, pp. 435-36; Mahesh C. Regmi, "Ferry-Points (Ghats) in Western Nepal," and "Ferry Services in Western Nepal," in *Regmi Research Series*, Year 19, Nos. 9-10, September-October 1987; and Year 19, No. 12, December 1987, pp. 173-74.

13. Cited in: Ludwig F. Stiller, *The Rise of the House of Gorkha*, 1975, p. 233.

14. Instructions to Subba Rudravir Shah of Kumaun, Shrawan badi 8, 1859 (July 1802), *RRC*, Vol. 24, p. 586; and to Kaji Ambar Simha Thapa, Baishakh badi 1, 1861 (May 1804), *RRC*, Vol. 19, p. 176.

15. Royal order to local authorities in the Trishuli-Kumaun region, Kartik badi 5, 1867 (October 1810), *RRC*, Vol. 39, p. 480.

16. Colonel Kirkpatrick, *An Account of the Kingdom of Nepaul*, 1969 (reprint of 1811 ed.), p. 39.

17. Royal order to local authorities between Kathmandu and Kumaun, Shrawan Badi 10, 1853 (July 1796), *RRC*, Vol. 23, p. 93; and Ashadh sudi 2, 1862 (June 1805), *RRC*, Vol. 6, pp. 285-86.

18. Royal order to the *subba* and other authorities on the Makawanpur-Chisapani route, Magh badi 4, 1856 (January 1800), *RRC*, Vol. 24, pp. 50-2; and Kartik sudi 7, 1868 (October 1811), *RRC*, Vol. 40, p. 297.

19. Royal order to *majhis* and *chaukidars* in the Kathmandu-Marsyangdi region, Ashadh badi 5, 1862 (June 1805), *RRC*, Vol. 6, p. 101.

20. The passport system for travelling through Chisapani remained in force until around 1953. *Nepal Gazette*, Year 1, No. 31, Falgun 27, 2008 (March 10, 1952); Year 1, No. 51, Shrawan 20, 2009 (August 4, 1952); Year 1, No. 28, Falgun 6, 2009 (February 17, 1953); *Gorkhapatra*, Jestha 17, 1984 (June 3, 1927) in *RSS*, Year 2, No. 5, May 1, 1970, p. 119.

21. Mahesh C. Regmi, *The State and Economic Surplus*, 1984, pp. 11-12.

22. Kirkpatrick, p. 56; Francis Hamilton, *An Account of the Kingdom of Nepal*, 1971 (reprint of 1819 ed.), pp. 196-97.

23. Royal order to Mahesh Upadhyaya, Jestha badi 1, 1856 (June 1799), *RRC*, Vol. 24, p. 733.

24. Stiller, p. 366.

25. David Bolt, *Gurkhas*, 1962, p. 58.

26. Cited in Mahesh C. Regmi, *An Economic History of Nepal*, 1846-1901, 1988, p. 21.

27. Royal order to Subba Dasharath Khatri and others, Falgun badi 30, 1862 (March 1806), *RRC*, Vol. 6, p. 733; and p. 107. Both these documents are dated Ashadh badi 5, 1862 (June 1805).

28. John Pemble, *The Invasion of Nepal*, 1971, p. 29.

29. Mahesh C. Regmi, *A Study in Nepali Economic History, 1768-1846*, 1971, pp. 103-9.

30. Esmomin, "Corvee", in *Encyclopaedia of the Social Sciences*, 1963, Vols. 3-4, pp. 455-57.

31. Raymond Leslie Buell, *"Forced Labor"*, do, Vol. 5-6, pp. 341-45.

32. Guralnik, p. 1120.

33. G.M. Trevelyan, *English Social History*, 1962 ed., pp. 347, and 458; Ramachandra Guha, *The Unquiet Woods*, 1989, pp. 25-27.

34. E.K. Pauw, *Report on the Tenth Settlement of the Garhwal District*, 1896, p. 52.

35. Separate royal orders to Kaji Nayan Simha Thapa, local authorities between Kathmandu and Garhwal, and *majhis* on the Trishuli and other rivers, Aswin 1862 (September 1805), *RRC*, Vol. 6, pp. 471-75 and 504-7.

36. Royal order to Khadga Khatri and Kripa Khawas regarding transportation of arms and ammunition from Kathmandu to Kumaun, Ashadh badi 7, 1862 (June 1805), *RRC*, Vol. 6, pp. 73-74.

37. Royal order to Dittha Bishram Khatri, regarding transportation of arms and ammunition of Kumaun, Aswin badi 11, 1862 (September1805), *RRC*, Vol. 6, pp. 480-81.

38. Royal order to local authorities in Pyuthan, Achham, Doti and Kumaun, Aswin badi 1, 1862 (September 1805), *RRC*, Vol. 6, pp. 435-36. The order was repeated two years later in August 1807, *RRC*, Vol. 6, pp. 1031-32.

39. Separate royal orders for different regions in the western region up to Garhwal, Aswin sudi 1, 1862 (September 1805), *RRC*, Vol.19, p. 262; Arrangements for safety of consignments of arms and ammunition, Aswin badi 12, 1862 (September, 1805), *RRC*, Vol. 6. pp. 471-72; Regulations for the Dharmathali-Kangra region, Poush badi 1, 1865 (December 1808), *RRC*, Vol. 36, pp. 196-200; do. for the Dharmathali-Jamuna region, Ashadh sudi 4, 1866 (June 1809), *RRC*, Vol. 40, pp. 65-72; do. for the Marsyangdi-Sutlej region, Bhadra sudi 6, 1868 (August 1811), *RRC*, Vol. 40, p. 262; Royal order to local authorities in areas west of the Bishnumati river in Kathmandu, Magh sudi 9, 1869 (January 1813), *RRC*, Vol. 39, p. 493.
40. Royal order to local authorities in the Dharmathali-Jamuna region, Magh badi 14, 1862 (January 1806), *RRC*, Vol. 6, pp. 719-20.
41. Royal orders to local authorities between Kathmandu and Kumaun, Ashadh badi 7, 1862 (June 1805), *RRC*, Vol. 6, p. 72; do. to Kaji Nayan Simha Thapa and Sardar Indra Simha Thapa, Aswin sudi 2, 1862 (September 1805), *RRC*, Vol. 6, pp. 506-7; do. to Dittha Bishram Khatri, Aswin sudi 2, 1862 (September 1805), *RRC*, Vol. 6, p. 504.
42. Separate royal orders to local authorities from Kathmandu to Kumaun, Baishakh badi 7, 1861 (April 1804), *RRC*, Vol. 5, pp. 468-69.
43. Instructions to Balabhadra and Dharmananda Khawas, Magh badi 4, 1863 (January 1807), *RRC*, Vol. 6, pp. 796-99.
44. *Hulak* services between Kathmandu and Kumaun, Shrawan badi 1, 1864 (July 1807), *RRC*, Vol. 20, pp. 429-39.
45. Instructions to Subedars Balabhadra Khatri and Dharmananda Khawas, Ashadh sudi 8, 1866 (June 1809), *RRC*, Vol. 40, pp. 65-72.
46. Instructions to Subedar Ranasur Thapa, Kartik badi 10, 1868 (October 1811), *RRC*, Vol. 40, pp. 283-86.
47. Mahesh Raj Panta, "Vira Bhakti Thapa" (The brave Bhakti Thapa), *Purnima*, Year 5, No. 1, Baisakh-Ashadh 2025 (April-June 1968), pp. 51-53.

48. Yogi Naraharinath, *Sandhipatrasangraha* (A collection of treaties and other documents), pp. 645-50.

49. Mahesh C. Regmi, *An Economic History of Nepal, 1846-1901*, pp. 25-26.

50. Royal order to Kaji Nayan Simha Thapa, Kartik badi 14, 1862 (October 1805), *RRC*, Vol. 6, pp. 634-36.

51. Royal order regarding ban on use of *hulak* facilities, Jestha badi 4, 1865 (May 1808), *RRC*, Vol. 36, pp. 81-82.

52. Royal order regarding ban on abuse of *hulak* facilities, Kartik badi 2, 1867 (October 1810), *RRC*, Vol. 39, p. 460.

53. Mahesh C. Regmi, *Land Tenure and Taxation in Nepal*, (1978 ed.), p. 511.

54. Instructions to Najki Nawal Simha and others, Marga badi 4, 1871 (November 1814), *RRC*, Vol. 41, pp. 441-6.

55. Mahesh C. Regmi, *Land Tenure and Taxation in Nepal*, pp. 513 and 530.

56. E.H. Carr, *What is History ?*, 1975, p. 81.

3

The Administration

The two main alternative functions of the political organization of a universal state are to maintain the supremacy of the empire-building power and to fill a political vacuum arising in the body social of the disintegrating society through the destruction or collapse of its former parochial states.

Arnold J. Toynbee[1]

For the Gorkhali rulers, it was easier to conquer territories than to govern them. Indeed, the Gorkhali elite, with their hill state background, were ill-equipped for the complex administrative task of controlling an 800-km stretch of Himalayan territory. They had little to fall back upon in the way of tradition or precedent, for the size and diversities of the Empire had no precedent in the region. The history of Gorkhali control of the subjugated territories was, therefore, marked by trial and error at every stage. These methods were based on two key instruments of imperial control: A provincial administration and a standing army. Both those instruments were Gorkhali creations, for none of the hill states had ever had the need or the means to maintain them. Chapter 3 describes the system of provincial administration, while Chapter 4 deals with the Gorkhali army, the main theme being their effectiveness or otherwise as instruments of imperial control.

General Observations

A note on the hierarchy of the political and administrative

elites in the state must precede the discussion. Traditionally, top-ranking leaders of the state were known as *bhardars*. The *bhardar* who occupied the topmost position in the hierarchy, invariably a member of the ruling Shah family, was known as *chautariya*. The *kaji*, who was of ministerial rank, came next in the list, while the *sardar*, who usually dealt with routine affairs of the administration or the army occupied the third place.[2] All these three categories of Gorkhali *bhardars* were represented in the provincial administration in Kumaun. The province also had the distinction of being the only one in the Empire which was under the administrative jurisdiction of a *chautariya*.

The Gorkhali administration in Kumaun, as elsewhere in the Empire, was based on individuals, rather than on institutions. No permanent government office was ever established there, and royal orders and directives were meant only for the *bhardars* to whom they were addressed. The Gorkhali administration was accordingly shaped by the status, personality, and influence of the *bhardars*.

The role of the *pajani* system in the Gorkhali administration and army must also be explained. Under that system, government employees of all categories, including *bhardars* and armymen, were screened every year. Those who passed the test were reconfirmed, transferred, or promoted, or else dismissed and replaced by new men, but were eligible for subsequent reappointment. In Kirkpatrick's words, the objective of the *pajani* system were:[3]

> to examine into the conduct of all the public officers during the preceding year, to degrade, punish, and reward them, according to their merits, and to bestow governments, military commands, and jaghire lands for the ensuing year, in all which it the policy of this court to make frequent changes, with the view of preventing local attachments, and the dangerous effects of long confirmed local authority; of accustoming its subjects to serve indifferently in all parts, and of keeping its

dependents always in a state fluctuating between hope and fear.

A *bhardar's* tenure in office was, therefore, uncertain and unpredictable. The system did not promote efficiency and even led *bhardars* to make the most of their brief and intermittent tenures for personal benefit.

The rulers seem to have realized the adverse impact of the *pajani* system on the morale and conduct of their employees. Accordingly, they made repeated attempts to make appointments for specified terms. In early 1793, they prescribed that all appointments in the Empire be made for an initial period of three years.[4] In 1803, *bhardars* in Kumaun were, similarly promised a three-year tenure.[5] These initiatives marked a clear departure from the traditional *pajani* system and were never actually implemented. On the contrary, the rulers appointed, transferred, promoted, or dismissed their employees whenever they liked.

Two Periods

The history of Gorkhali administration in Kumaun may be divided into two distinct periods: The non-war years from 1791 to 1804, when the Gorkhali state's campaign of territorial expansion remained in suspension, and the war years from 1804 to 1815. Since it is the nature of the affairs of state that determines the nature of the administration[6] the needs and responsibilities of the Gorkhali state in Kumaun were different during the times of peace and the times of war.

(a) The Non-War Years (1791-1804)

During this period, the provincial administration was headed by a *bhardar* with the title of *subba* or governor. British sources have described the *subba* as "governors of districts,"[7] or "an officer of revenue, justice, and police".[8] He represented the Gorkhali power in the province, combining at least three different roles. He was:

(1) Chief of the civil administration.

(2) Chief of the revenue administration responsible for collection and disbursement of revenue. He also functioned as a tax-farmer, entitled to appropriate surplus revenue for himself.

(3) A representative of the Gorkhali state in dealing with foreign states.

Kumaun was governed by as many as eleven *subbas* during the 14-year period until 1804, an average of about 15 months each. Because of their high status, changes in the central political leadership inevitably led to changes in the provincial administration. It is indeed significant that during the four-year period of ex-King Ran Bahadur Shah's exile in India, there were as many as three *subbas* in Kumaun, and that two of them remained in that post for less than ten months each. The period for which the *subbas* actually worked in Kumaun was shorter, because it was seldom possible for them to join their duty immediately after their appointment.

The functions and powers of the Kathmandu-appointed *subbas* were defined in their letters of appointment, regulations, and other documents issued under the seal of the reigning Gorkhali King. The nature and extent of those functions and powers changed according to the changing political situation and the territorial ambitions of the Gorkhali leaders. These documents, however, should be taken with caution. They are more important as a reflection of the mind of the rulers in Kathmandu than as guidelines for the local authorities which were seriously implemented. The brief periods for which they worked in Kumaun, and their tendency to make the most of their term for personal benefit, made implementation nothing more than an issue of academic interest. One may also question the feasibility of implementing the central instructions with the manpower available to the local authorities, even with the best of intentions.

There is little point in describing the powers and

functions of all the nine men who worked as *subba* in Kumaun between 1791 and 1804. Several of them emerge as shadowy figures with uneventful terms, although this may be due to gaps in documentation. I shall, therefore, limit myself to the main highlights of the administrative system during that 14-year period.

For nearly two years after the conquest, Kumaun remained a victim of administrative confusion in which loot, plunder, and killings were the order of the day. Jog Narayan Malla, one of the commanders of the victorious army, had been designated as *subba* of the province, but seems to have been powerless to do anything. It was against this background that in January 1793 the Regent, Bahadur Shah, appointed Nar Shah as *subba* of Kumaun. His appointment came less than four months after the end of the wars with Tibet and China. During the months that followed, the political scenario in Kathmandu changed, and the position of the Regent, Bahadur Shah, became shaky. The Gorkhali leaders were hardly in a position to continue the campaign of territorial expansion beyond Kumaun. Regulations defining the functions and powers of Nar Shah, promulgated in January 1793, reflect these constraints. His main functions were to collect revenues from prescribed sources, and use the proceeds to pay the salaries of Gorkhali troops in Kumaun, comprising a total of 400 fighting men, as well as of local functionaries. He was also required to construct and repair forts, manufacture gunpowder and other ammunition, develop mines, confiscate tax-free land grants without valid titles, and punish rebels and other criminals with death, if appropriate. These were all routine and mundane tasks of provincial administration. Only one section reflects the security concerns of the rulers: "In the event of invasion by enemies from any side, recruit the necessary troops, and repulse the invasion."[9] The emphasis was on defense rather on territorial expansion.

A British source has described Nar Shah's administration as "marked by great cruelties and excesses."

It has also mentioned a "massacre" of selected groups of people of Kumaun on his orders: "Once he assembled people of the Nagarkoti community, who used to work as mercenary troops of the former rulers of Kumaun, at one place on the pretext of a population census. The source adds: "He then arranged that on a night agreed upon and at a given signed they should be slaughtered without mercy. His instructions were carried out".[10] Official Nepali sources corroborate this account. Orders issued by Ran Bahadur in 1794-95 admit that the *bhardars* had subjected the Nagarkoti community to severe hardships, and that 'Nar Shah had greatly oppressed the people of Kumaun."[11]

In May 1794, King Ran Bahadur Shah, who had already come of age, dismissed the Regent, his uncle Bahadur Shah, and took over the administration. Chapter 1 has noted how he followed an aggressive imperialist policy and started making preparations for renewing the campaign of territorial expansion. Reorganization of the administrative system in the trans-Marsyangdi region formed part and parcel of those preparations. In July 1794, that is, within three months after taking over the administration, Ran Bahadur appointed Ajav Khawas as *subba* in Kumaun and designated Bhakti Thapa, a *sardar*, to oversee administrative and military matters in the region. A summary of the royal instructions to the *sardar* is given below:[12]

> In the event of external aggression, spend the amounts needed to repulse it. Receive envoys of rulers of different states, and send them to Kathmandu if appropriate. Rulers of vassal and other states in the region shall comply with your orders and perform their duties at the places assigned by you. People who rebel against the Gorkhali rule shall be punished with death, imprisonment, or otherwise, according to the gravity of their crimes, but their families shall not be enslaved.

Bhakti Thapa was also granted *pajani* authority over Kumaun in consultation with the *subba*. Bhakti Thapa's appointment as chief of a regional set-up reflects poor judgment on the part of King Ran Bahadur Shah. His territorial jurisdiction was extensive, covering a number of provinces, including Jumla and Kumaun, which were administered by *bhardars* of higher rank and influence. There were also vassal states such as Bajhang, Bajura and Jajarkot, which were administered by their own autonomous rulers. Such a set-up hardly contributed to cooperation and coordination. Bhakti Thapa accordingly faced non-cooperation from the *subba* and other Gorkhalis in Kumaun from the very beginning. The tactless manner in which he exercised his *pajani* authority by dismissing the relatives of the central authorities was yet another minus point in his record. For a man who was basically a soldier, the intricacies of decision-making were indeed baffling.

Bhakti Thapa's duties in the trans-Marsyangdi region were thus confined to the military and diplomatic fields. To fill the gap in revenue administration, Ran Bahadur Shah designated Bam Shah, a *chautariya*. His duties were to revise revenue assessments in the region; a task which he completed by April 1796.[13]

In early 1795, Ran Bahadur appointed Amar Simha Thapa as *subba* of the province. Soon after his appointment, Amar led an attack on a strip of Tarai territory in the south, which once belonged to Kumaun but had passed into the control of the Nawab of Avadh before the Gorkhali conquest. The action was contrary to Kathmandu's express orders. Moreover, Amar Thapa did not consider it necessary to inform Bhakti Thapa in advance. Ran Bahadur realized that the incident had taken place mainly because of shortcomings in the Gorkhali administrative set-up in Kumaun. In his view, the Gorkhali *bhardars* in Kumaun, instead of working unanimously in the interests of the *dhungo*, "harmed relations with the British as well as with the Nawab." Consequently, he added, the administration of Kumaun had become a victim of neglect. In his words: "Because the *subba* (Amar Thapa) and the *sardar* (Bhakti Thapa) could not work together in Kumaun, no attention was paid to the administration of the province."

Ran Bahadur then made the following changes in the Gorkhali administrative set-up in Kumaun. He dismissed Amar Thapa and appointed Bam Shah as chief of the provincial administration. Until the arrival of Bam Shah, Bhakti Thapa was retained in Kumaun, but his *pajani* authority was withdrawn. He was also ordered to discharge his duties only in consultation with Bam Shah and his *sardar* deputy. The Gorkhali officers in the vassal state of Garhwal were granted authority to look after the administration of Kumaun on a provisional basis.

These interim arrangements lasted only a few months. In early 1796, Ran Bahadur Shah appointed Prabal Rana as *subba* of Kumaun in the vacancy caused by the dismissal of Amar Thapa.[14]

In August 1796, Ran Bahadur Shah unearthed a corruption scandal involving several *kajis* and other *bhardars*. It appeared that they had sent a Brahmin, Kulanidhi Tiwari, to Bhirkot, a western hill territory which had recently been brought under central administration, to collect the coronation tax without royal authority. Kulanidhi shared the money with his co-conspirators. Ran Bahadur Shah punished the Brahmin with degradation to the lowest caste and banished him. The *bhardars*, on their part, were made to pay to the government twice the amount they had received, plus a fine of Rs. 100 each. The erring *bhardars*, included Prabal Rana. He was found to have taken Rs. 500 so he was ordered to pay the government a total sum of Rs. 1,100.[15]

Ran Bahadur deputed Bam Shah to investigate the situation in Kumaun, check revenue collections made by Prabal Rana in Kumaun, and recommend reforms. Bam Shah recommended that the post of *subba* be abolished and Kumaun's administration be taken over by the center. In his opinion, such a step would lead to an increase in revenue, which could be used to meet military and other expenses in the province, and even generate a surplus. In January 1797 Ran Bahadur accepted the recommendation, dismissed Prabal Rana, and replaced him by Bam Shah himself. Ran

Bahadur granted Bam Shah broad authority in the administration of Kumaun:[16]

> We have granted you authority to make necessary arrangements regarding war, peace, and administration in that territory. Do what is necessary to promote our cause and bring credit to yourself. Keep the people satisfied and ensure that no complaints are received here and the territory remains prosperous.

Ram Shah's *sardar* assistants, Indrabir Simha and Amar Simha Thapa, were similarly instructed in September 1797:[17]

> We had previously granted to *chautariya* Bam Shah full authority over the administration of Kumaun. We hereby reconfirm his authority. In matters relating to war and peace, as well as *pajani*, do what will serve our interests and bring credit to you through consultations among all three of you.

Bam Shah's role came to an end some time in 1798, when Ajav Khawas, who had worked as *subba* of Kumaun in 1794-95 was reappointed in that province.[18]

In July 1802, Kathmandu made a new experiment in the administration of Kumaun. Instead of appointing a single *bhardar* as *subba*, it divided the post between two brothers of the same *bhardar's* family. The reasons for such an experiment are not clear. The experiment at least enabled Kathmandu to employ two *bhardars* for the cost of one, because they had to split the salary and perquisites of one *subba* between themselves. Under the new order, the two brothers of Bam Shah, namely, Rudravir and Hastadal, were appointed as *co-subba* of Kumaun in July 1802. They were succeeded by Gajakesar and Ranakesar Pande—sons of Chief Kaji, Damodar Pande, in April 1803. The experiment apparently did not yield the expected benefits and was therefore abandoned.[19]

The situation in Kumaun changed after King Ran Bahadur abdicated and went into exile in India in 1800. After a brief lull, the imperial ambitions of the Gorkhali leaders started becoming manifest once again, as reflected in regulations issued to Subba Rudravir Shah that were reissued with almost no change to his successors.[20] There are two sets of these regulations, one set in the name of the *subbas*, and the other in the names of the *subbas* and his *sardar* assistants. A summary of the first set of regulations is given below:[21]

> Persuade people who have fled from Kumaun to come back and make the province populous. Collect the revenue in consultation with local functionaries. Replace disobedient officers with more capable persons. Construct and repair forts and *sanghus* in the province. Punish Gorkhalis and other persons who confess to any crime with death or otherwise.

Indeed, the *subba* was granted broad powers to take any action in accordance with these regulations "that serves the interests of the Gorkhali state, promotes our cause, facilitates the collection of revenue, makes the province prosperous, and brings credit to you."

The second set of regulations deals with foreign relations and the internal political affairs of the vassal state of Garhwal. The main points are summarized below:

> Remain prepared to resist external aggression, if any, but do not engage in any aggression from our side. If the enemy invades our territory, defend our headquarters, and strike at him where he is weakest. If your forces prove insufficient, recruit additional troops.
>
> Engage in regular correspondence with the English, the Nawab (of Oudh), and the Sikhs, the Marathas, and other powers in the western region. In consultation with the ruler of Garhwal, engage in similar correspondence with the rulers of the western principalities, including Sirmur and Kangra. Ascertain how many rulers side with Kangra, how many are opposed to it, and how many will support us if we proceed westward.

> Resolve boundary disputes with Garhwal in consultation with old and informed people of both sides. If the two sides do not agree, retain the line of actual occupation on either side, and refer the matter to us. In case there arise internal disputes in Garhwal, settle them in such a way that the interests of the Gorkhali state are served and promoted. In case a request is made for mediation, send capable men to negotiate a settlement, if possible. If the ruler of Garhwal face any threat from any source, summon him, or his brother, or the Crown Prince, whoever is considered most suitable, to Almora, and provide assistance to him if the threat is real. Otherwise, do whatever is necessary that serves the interests of the state and proves your loyalty.

The regulations also empowered the *subba* to allocate sources of income to leaders from Kumaun and Garhwal who were willing to come over to the Gorkhali side.

On his return to Kathmandu in March 1804, Ran Bahadur took a number of steps which had a profound impact on the administration of Kumaun. He dismissed the incumbent *subba*, Gajakesar Pande. No new *subba* was appointed to replace him, and the post became defunct. The man Ran Bahadur chose to head Kumaun's new administrative set-up was Ambar Simha Thapa. (not to be confused with Amar Simha Thapa, the *subba*). In April 1804, Ambar was appointed chief administrator of Kumaun with more or less the same functions, duties, and responsibilities as the *subba*.[22] But he did not remain long in Kumaun. The pace of Gorkhali military activity soon led to the enlargement of his role in the administration of the region and the Gorkhali army on the western front. It was under his command that Garhwal was finally annexed in late 1804. It was also under his command that the Gorkhalis crossed the Sutlej river and laid siege to the fort of Kangra. In September 1805, Ambar was appointed chief administrator of the Kangra region, a post he shared with Bhimsen Thapa's brother, Nayan Simha Thapa.[23] He was also granted *pajani* authority in the territories west of the Marsyangdi river.[24] In November 1806, the two *bhardars* were given *mukhtiyar* authority to decide on issues of war and peace on the western front.[25] This marked the end of Ambar Thapa's direct role in Kumaun, although his authority to oversee Kumaun's administration continued. He was thus the supreme commander of the western front, rather than a mere provincial administrator in Kumaun. Meanwhile, routine administrative functions in Kumaun were handled by *bhardars* of *sardar* rank, or by military commanders.[26]

(b) The War Years (1804-15)

Important changes were made in Kumaun's administration after Ambar Thapa was elevated to the status of Supreme Commander of the western front. The campaign of imperialist expansion was resumed with the annexation of Garhwal in October 1804. The policies and programmes of the Gorkhali rulers were thereafter attuned to the needs of the military campaign. The new set-up, which remained in place until the end of Gorkhali rule in Kumaun, had two main aspects. Firstly, Kumaun was treated as one unit in a regional set-up. The practice of appointing a *subba* as chief of the province was discontinued. Secondly, the civil administration was separated from the revenue administration and was run by *bhardars* of *sardar* rank under the ultimate control of Ambar Thapa. The revenue administration was placed under the jurisdiction of other *bhardars*, either in their individual capacity or as members of teams. I shall here discuss those arrangements only from the administrative viewpoint, leaving matters relating to revenue assessment, collection, and assignations or disbursements for Chapter 5 (The Revenue System) and Chapter 6 (The Jagir System).

In mid-June 1805, the central authorities deputed teams to different regions of the empire to check tax-free land grants and register undeclared lands. One of the team was sent to Kumaun under Kaji Ritudhwaj Khawas. The size of the team may be regarded as an index of the importance it was given by the Gorkhali authorities at the center. It was comprised of at least 16 members, including the *kaji*, and 14 surveyors from Kathmandu.[27] Unlike the other teams, it was also given revenue functions. Its main function was to prescribe the amount of revenue assessment in each district of the province in such a manner that "revenue does not decline, and tax-payers accept the assessment." The team was granted authority to scrutinize revenue collections since the Gorkhali conquest, and find out how much revenue was collected from the people, how much was handed over to the authorities, and how much was embezzled. It was also ordered to ascertain the amount of assessment during the Chand rule, and the changes made by the Gorkhalis. The team also assigned sources of revenue to the Gorkhali armymen in Kumaun in lieu of salaries according to schedules prescribed by the central authorities.[28]

The work done by *kaji* Ritudhwaj Khawas in Kumaun laid the foundation of a new system of revenue administration in that province. Meanwhile, the political situation in Kathmandu changed. Ran Bahadur Shah was assassinated in April 1806. Ritudhwaj Khawas was summoned back to Kathmandu, but was executed in Doti while on his way.[29] His brother, Kaji Tribhuwan Khawas, had already been executed in Kathmandu.

In June 1807, Bam Shah was again deputed to the trans-Bheri region under the overall supervision of *Kaji* Ambar Thapa. He remained there until April 1815, when he surrendered to the British on the conclusion of the Gorkha-Britain war.[30] Bam Shah was helped by two senior *kajis*, namely, Rewant Kunwar, and Hastadal Shah, his own brother. None of these three *bhardars* had jurisdiction over Kumaun alone. Rather, they were given specific assignments in the trans-Bheri province, particularly in Doti, Kumaun and Garhwal, from time to time.[31]

Bam Shah's second term as administrator in Kumaun has been acclaimed by British sources. In their opinion, his administration was "one of the best" in the Gorkhali Empire, and "matters changed very much for the better" in Kumaun. They add:[32]

> Garhwal was at this time governed as if its rulers' sole object was to turn it again into a jungle, but Kumaun appears to have been favoured in every way. The property of private individuals was respected, the grants of land made by previous rulers were confirmed to the actual possessors, the revenue was collected in the usual manner, a rude attempt to administer justice was made, and most prized of all it was forbidden to sell the persons of revenue-defaulters and their families into slavery.

But these steps do not seen to have benefitted the peasants of Kumaun by mitigating their tax and other burdens in any way, nor could the ban on enslavement be effective. The discriminatory treatment allegedly suffered by Garhwal is also difficult to explain, since Bam Shah exercised overall jurisdictions over both territories.

The Gorkhali retreat to the region east of the Sutlej river after the failure of the four-year siege of the Kangra fort in 1809 was a momentous event in the history of the Empire. To be sure, this event by no means led to the cessation of military activity in the Sutlej region. Indeed, it was at that time that such states in that region as Sirmur and Besahar were annexed. But those were relatively minor campaigns for the Gorkhalis, and some of those states actually fell without a fight.[33] Moreover, the Gorkhalis kept alive their plans to conquer Kangra. But the retreat also provided a respite which they used for improving the administration.

Three steps taken on a single day—October 19, 1810, show this well. A senior *kaji*, Balnarsimha Kunwar, was ordered to check assignations of sources of revenue to Gorkhali military companies, resume surplus sources, if any, and also meet shortfalls. Another duty was to arrange for the reclamation of uncultivated lands of all tenure categories.[34] Sardar Bakhat Simha Basnyat was assigned the duty of scrutinizing accounts and records of revenue collection throughout the Empire.[35] In October 1811, the functions and duties of these two Gorkhali *bhardars* were combined and placed under the jurisdiction of *kaji* Bir Kesar Pande.[36] However, it is not possible to judge the impact of those steps on the Gorkhali administration in Kumaun and other province.

It was also on October 19, 1810 that the Gorkhali rulers set up a new layer of administrative authority in the Bheri-Jamuna region. The reasons for that step are not clear, since Bam Shah was already working there. It is possible the objective was to impose a check on the *chautariya*'s authority. This impression is substantiated by the fact that Kathmandu's instructions contain no reference to Bam Shah's role. The new layer was headed by Kaji Bahadur Bhandari (assisted by Bakshi Dasharath Khatri) in 1810-12, and by Kaji Bakhtawar Simha Basnet after 1812. Its functions and duties were more or less the same as those of the *subbas* of the non-war period. They included appropriate steps to check external aggression and internal rebellion, supervise collection, assignation, or disbursement of revenue, confiscate irregular tax-free land grant and check depopulation. It was also given authority to check enslavement of the people and punish people who violated caste and communal sanctions and strictures. These issues will be discussed in Chapter 7 (The People of Kumaun).

Role of the Center

With at least two administrative tiers at the provincial and regional levels, it would be legitimate to believe that the Gorkhali rulers would have used those tiers in dealing with local functionaries and common people in Kumaun. However, this was by no means the case. Kathmandu dealt directly with them whenever it wanted to do so, by-passing the Gorkhali authorities in the province and the region. Such a policy further worsened the administrative confusion.

There were several reasons for direct central intervention in the administration of Kumaun. Firstly, Kathmandu never delegated its power to appoint local revenue functionaries to the provincial or regional authorities. Secondly, it appointed official teams from time to time to inspect facilities, such as ferry services on rivers, transport and communications, and forts and other military installations. Thirdly, it deputed high-power commissions to Kumaun to implement such empire-wide programmes as the confiscation of tax-free lands with defective or no title-deeds. At times, such teams were sent to study the performance of the provincial administration, particularly in matters relating to the collection of revenue. Finally, the Gorkhali rulers maintained an open door for any complaint from any person in any part of the Empire. In early 1812, a judicial officer was appointed at the Royal Palace in Kathmandu with the following duties:[37]

> Give a proper hearing to any person from anywhere in the territories of Gorkha who complains of oppression and injustice by *bhardars* or other employees or armymen. Refer such complaints to us along with your opinion and take action according to our orders. Let not any complainant go back because of delay is disposing of his complaint lest he should tell others: "I had gone to the Royal Palace to complain of injustice, but no one listened to me."

The facility of such direct access to the central authorities is Kathmandu was frequently used for the redress of grievances, particularly by the subject populations of the Empire.

Administrative Shortcomings

This account of the Gorkhali administration in Kumaun should not lead to the conclusion that it was under the effective control of Kathmandu. This was by no means the case. The tenuous transport and communication links, which made two-way communication a matter of several weeks, was in itself enough to make remote control and supervision by the central authorities largely ineffective. Royal orders issued from Kathmandu had little effect on what the *bhardars* did in the light of the actual situation on the ground and their own interests. This may partly explain why the Gorkhali rulers followed a lenient policy toward *bhardars* found guilty of incompetence, corruption, or oppression. For instance, Dhaukal Simha Basnyat had worked as *subba* of Morang during 1793-97. He had then subjected the local people to illegal taxation and even intruded into the jurisdiction of fellow *bhardars,* for which he had received a severe reprimand from Kathmandu. Nevertheless, he was deputed to Kumaun as *subba* in April 1800.[38] Amar Simha Thapa was removed from the post of *subba* in the aftermath of the misguided attack on the territories of the Nawab of Avadh in 1796. However, he remained in Kumaun for several years thereafter in the capacity of *sardar* under Bam Shah.[39]

Conflicting or overlapping administrative jurisdiction was an equally serious shortcoming of the Gorkhali administrative system. It had at least two levels: One between the provincial and regional administrators and the other between Kathmandu and the regional administrators. As previously noted, the Bhandari-Khatri team was deputed to the Bheri-Jamuna region in October 1810 at a time when Bam Shah, Rewant Kunwar, and Hastadal Shah were already there. Royal instructions to the team, however, do not mention the fact. There is one reference to Hastadal Shah which prescribed that Hastadal should collect the revenue and hand over the proceeds to Bahadur Bhandari, while Dasharath Khatri should keep accounts and records.[40] This may mean that the central authorities had anticipated a conflict of jurisdiction.

But that step did not resolve the problem in full, for there were many other areas of conflict. For example, in early 1813, judicial officers appointed by the Bhandari-Khatri team were told that their duty should be restricted to investigations only, and that they were not entitled to collect fines and penalties. The royal order adds:[41]

> "We have granted authority to chautariya Bam Shah and Subba Hastadal Shah to administer justice in territories assigned to Gorkhali companies in Kumaun, collect fines and penalties and use the income to meet shortfalls of income resulting from damage to land or crops by floods and landslides, or non-cultivation, and pay allowances to the troops."

The officers were strictly ordered not to interfere in these functions of the *chautariya*.

Concluding Remarks

The *modus operandi* of imperial control in Kumaun was complex and convoluted. It was based on what may be called the policy of overlapping jurisdictions. Various layers of administrative and supervisory jurisdictions were created for the province and the region, but those jurisdictions, although formally separate, jutted into one another in important fields. The result was that separate administrative and supervisory authorities, although deriving their powers from the center, faced obstructions at every step from their fellow authorities. Such confusion prevented the Gorkhali *bhardars* from exercising absolute authority in the province, but made the provincial and regional administration weak and ineffective. How to check leakage of revenue, supervise transport and communication links, and prevent the local Gorkhali authorities from oppressing and exploiting the people was, consequently, a no less formidable task at the end of the Gorkhali rule than it was at the time of the conquest.

NOTES

1. Arnold J. Toynbee, *A Study of History*, 1965, Vol. 2, p. 45.
2. Mahesh C. Regmi, *Kings and Political Leaders of the Gorkhali Empire, 1768-1814*, 1995, pp. 40-41.
3. Colonel Kirkpatrick, *An Account of the Kingdom of Nepaul*, 1811, pp. 197-201; Regmi, pp. 41-42.

4. Mahesh C. Regmi, *A Study in Nepali Economic History, 1768-1846*, 1971, p. 201.

5. Royal instructions to Subba Rudravir Shah for Kumaun, Shrawan badi 8, 1859 (July 1802), *RRC*, Vol. 24, p. 579.

6. Leonard D. White, "Administration", *Encyclopaedia of the Social Sciences*, 1963 ed., Vols. 1-2, p. 440.

7. Kirkpatrick, p. 202.

8. Francis Hamilton, *An Accou t of the Kingdom of Nepal*, 1819, p. 105.

9. Regulations for Kumaun, Kartik badi 2, 1867 (October 1810), *RRC*, Vol. 39, p. 449; Appointment of Nar Shah as *Subba* of Kumaun and royal instructions, Poush sudi 13, 1849 (January 1793), *RRC*, Vol. 5, pp. 234-39; *Regmi Research Series*, Year 4, No. 4, April 1, 1972, p. 61, and Year 4, No. 9, September 1, 1972, pp. 171-72.

10. Edwin T. Atkinson, *The Himalayan Districts of the North-Western Provinces of India*, 1882, Vol. 2, p. 623.

11. Royal order to Jagat Bisht, Falgun sudi 15, 1852 (March 1796), *RRC*, Vol. 5, p. 312; do. to the *Kamins* of *Chyudi*, Shrawan badi 8, 1851 (July 1794), do. p. 183; *Regmi Research Series*, Year 4, No. 4, April 1972, pp. 61-64.

12. These instructions, and other information about Bhakti Thapa, are contained in Mahesh Raj Pant, "Vira Bhakti Thapa" (The Brave Bhakti Thapa), *Purnima*, Year 3, No. 2, Shrawan 1, 2023 (July 1966) and following issues.

13. Royal order to Chautariya Bam Shah and Sardar Indrabir, Baisakh badi 2, 1853 (April 1796), *RRC*, Vol. 19, p. 104.

14. No 12 above.

15. Regmi, *Kings and Political Leaders*, pp. 58-59.

16. Royal order to Chautariya Bam Shah, Magh badi 14, 1853 (January 1797), *RRC*, Vol. 5, p. 353; *Regmi Research Series*, Year 4, No. 4, April 1, 1972, P. 64.

17. Royal order to Sardars Indrabir Simha and Amar Simha Thpa, Aswin badi 13, 1854 (September 1797), *RRC*, Vol. 25, p. 634.

18. Appointment of Ajav Khawas as Subba of Kumaun, Shrawan badi 8, 1851 (July 1794), *RRC*, Vol. 5, p. 183, *RRS*, Year 4, No. 4, April 1, 1972, p. 64; No. 12 above.

19. Separate regulations for (a) Subba Rudrabir Shah, and (b) Subba Rudravir Shah and Sardars Puran Shah and Bhairav Simha, Shrawan badi 8, 1859 (July 1802), *RRC*, Vol. 24, pp. 571-85; Royal order to Subba Rudrabir Shah to hand over charge to Gajakesar and Ranakesar Pande, Chaitra sudi 13, 1859, (April 1803), *RRC*, Vol. 5, P. 378; *RRS*, Year 4, No. 4, April 1, 1972, pp. 64-65; Appointment of Gajakesar and Ranakesar Pande as co-Subbas of Kumaun and regulations, Ashadh badi 9, 1860 (June 1803), *RRC*, Vol. 20, pp. 87-90; *RRS*, Year 4, No. 5, May 1, 1972, pp. 87-90.

20. Royal instructions to Kaji Ambar Simha Thapa regarding administration of Kumaun, Baisakh badi 1, 1891 (April 1804), *RRC*, Vol. 19, pp. 174-80.

21. do. to Kajis Ambar Simha Thapa and Nayan Simha Thapa regarding preparations for the Kangra campaign, Aswin sudi 2, 1862 (September 1805), *RRC*, Vol. 6, pp. 515-16.

22. Royal order to Kaji Ambar Simha Thapa and Sardar Ranjit Kunwar, Aswin sudi 12, 1862 (September 1805), *RRC*, Vol. 6, p. 124.

23. Mahesh Raj Pant, "Vira Bhakti Thapa" (The brave Bhakti Thapa), *Purnima*, No. 17, Baisakh-Ashadh, 2025 (April-June 1968), p. 53; Atkinson, Vol. 2 pp. 616-20.

24. Royal orders to (1) Subedar Chhirbire Khawas, Chaitra sudi 13, 1862 (March 1806), *RRC*, Vol. 6, p. 759, (2) Sardars Nath Padhya and Ransur Thapa, Falgun sudi 2, 1869 (February 1813), *RRC*, Vol. 39, P. 500.

25. Royal notifications regarding appointment of Kaji Ritudhwaj Khawas in Kumaun, Jestha sudi 5, 1862 (May 1805), *RRC*, Vol. 5, pp. 521-25; *RRS*, Year 4, No. 4, April 1, 1972, pp. 65-66.

26. Royal instructions to Kaji Ritudhwaj Khawas for Kumaun, Jestha sudi 3, 1862 (May 1805), *RRC*, Vol. 5, pp. 526-35.

27. Atkinson, p. 616.

28. do.

29. Royal order to Chautariya Bam Shah regarding enslavement in Garhwal, Ashadh badi 10, 1864 (April 1807), *RRC*, Vol. 20, p. 404; Royal order to Chautariya Bam Shah regarding report that he had taken over charge of Garhwal but not yet of Kumaun, Shrawan sudi 4, 1064 (July 1807), *RRC*, Vol. 20, p. 465; Royal order to Kaji Rewant Kunwar regarding supply of elephants from Pyuthan, Kartik badi 2, 1864 (October 1807), *RRC*, Vol. 6, p. 1052; Royal order to Subbas of Garhwal regarding salary of Chautariya Bam Shah, Baisakh sudi 3, 1865 (April 1808), *RRC*, Vol. 36, p. 76; Royal order to Kaji Ambar Simha Thapa for deputing one company to Chautariya Bam Shah in Kumaun, Baisakh sudi 3, 1865 (May 1808), *RRC*, Vol. 36, p. 76; Royal notification regarding Kaji Rewant Kunwar's appointment in Kumaun, Jestha sudi 13, 1865, (May 1808), *RRC*, Vol. 36, p. 114; Royal order to Chautariya Bam Shah and Kaji Rewant Kunwar regarding enslavement in Kumaun, Aswin badi 8, 1865 (September 1808), *RRC*, Vol. 36, pp. 165-66; Royal order to Chautariya Bam Shah and Kaji Rewant Kunwar to pay allowances to troops from the revenues of Kumaun, Chaitra badi 2, 1865 (March 1809), *RRC*, Vol. 36, p. 242; Royal order to Chautariya Bam Shah and Kaji Rewant Kunwar regarding restoration of villages in Phaldakot, Kumaun, to Bhawani Shankar Pant, Shrawan badi 1, 1867 (July 1810), *RRC*, Vol. 39, p. 276; Royal order to Subba Hastadal Shahi for Doon region, Shrawan badi 10, 1867 (July 1810), *RRC*, Vol. 9, pp. 282-87; Royal confirmation of Kaji Rewant Kunwar's authority in Kumaun, Marga 9, 1866 (November 24, 1810), *RRC*, Vol. 40, p. 123; Royal order appointing Subba Hastadal Shah in the Doon region, Shrawan badi 7, 1867 (July 1810), *RRC*, Vol. 39, pp. 288-89; Royal order to Kaji Rewant Kunwar regarding administration in Garhwal and Sirmur, Bhadra sudi 5, 1867 (August 1810), *RRC*, Vol. 39, pp. 381-89; Royal order regarding Kaji Rewant Kunwar's powers to take action against army deserters in the trans-Bheri region, Marga sudi 10, 1868 (December 1811), *RRC*, Vol. 40, p. 317; Royal order to Chautariya Bam Shah and Subba Hastadal Shah regarding salaries of

companies, Marga sudi 15, 1868 (December 1811), *RRC*, Vol. 40, p. 318.

30. Hamilton, p. 298; Atkinson, p. 624.

31. L.F Stiller, *The Rise of the House of Gorkha*, 1975, pp. 240-42; Notification in the Mahakali-Sutlej region regarding preparations for the Besahar campaign, Magh sudi 3, 1867 (January 1811), *RRC*, Vol. 38, pp. 715-17.

32. Royal order to Kaji Balnarsimha Kunwar, Kartik 10, 1867 (October 19, 1810), *RRC*. Vol. 38. pp. 591-93; An identical order was issued to Kaji Birkesar Pande on the same day, *RRC*, Vol. 40, pp. 307-8.

33. Royal order to Sardar Bakhat Simha Basnyat, Kartik 10, 1867 (October 19, 1810), *RRC*, Vol. 38, pp. 593-94.

34. Royal orders and instructions to Kaji Birkesar Pande, Kartik sudi 7, 1868 (November 1811), *RRC*, Vol. 40, pp, 296-97; Poush badi 30, 1868 (January 1812), *RRC*, Vol. 40, pp. 327-28; Falgun sudi 1, 1868 (February 1812), do., pp. 383-86.

35. Royal instructions to Kaji Bahadur Bhandari and Bakshi Dasharath Khatri, Kartik badi 2, 1867 (October 1810), *RRC*, Vol. 39, pp. 449-59.

36. do. to Kaji Bakhtawar Simha Basnyat, Poush badi 12, 1869 (December 1812), *RRC*, Vol. 41, pp. 188-91.

37. Royal instructions to Birbhadra Kunwar, Magh sudi 5, 1868 (January 1813), *RRC*, Vol. 40, pp. 358-62.

38. Regmi, *Kings and Political Leaders*, pp. 39-40.

39. Note No. 17 above.

40. Note No. 35 above.

41. Royal order to *bicharis* in Kumaun, Chaitra badi 12, 1867 (March 1811), *RRC*, Vol. 41, p. 51.

4

The Gorkhali Army

Such princes and republics of modern times as have no national troops for defense or attack ought well to be ashamed of it; for they should bear in mind that their not having armies of their own is not from the want of men fit for military services, but that the fault is wholly theirs, in not knowing how to make soldiers of their men. And there is nothing more true than that, if there are no soldiers where there are men, it is not owing to any natural or local defect, but is solely the fault of the prince.

Niccolo Machiavelli (1469-1527)[1]

The Gorkhali military presence in Kumaun was a natural corollary of the conquest of that territory. From the viewpoint of the Gorkhali rulers, such a presence was needed to defend Kumaun from external aggression, maintain law and order, and facilitate further military campaigns toward the west. However, an army is not only a military organization, it is also a symbol of national or imperial power. The size and character of armies are, therefore, largely determined by a nation's real necessities as developed by history and enforced by circumstances.[2] This Chapter describes the origin and composition of the armed forces of the Gorkhali state and their deployment in different parts of the Gorkhali Empire, with a special emphasis on the province of Kumaun.

The Background

The successes of the Gorkhali state in its campaign of imperial expansion were due to the fact that unlike other states in the Himalayan region, it possessed a standing army, that is, an army maintained on a permanent basis in peacetime as well as in times of war.[3] The establishment of a standing army was an innovation of far-reaching significance, for none of the states of the Himalayan region had any such army.[4]

How did the Gorkhalis fight their battles before the formation of a standing army ? The hill states of the Himalayan region, including Gorkha and Kumaun, lacked the resources to maintain standing armies. At the same time, they needed to maintain forces of fighting men to defend their territories against hostile neighbours, or take part in expansionist campaigns of their own. Accordingly, they maintained fighting men on a regular basis without any formal organization. In grave situations, these forces were reinforced by fresh enlistments from the local population. For instance, for the invasion of Kathmandu in 1768, Prithvi Narayan Shah enlisted "healthy and able-bodied men between 15 and 30 years of age, strong and brave, active and alert, who can fight with their chests as shields.[15] Similarly, in early 1791, when the Gorkhalis invaded Kumaun, the ruler, Mahendra Chand "summoned the entire fighting population" and also used "part of his regular troops.[6]

The Militia

Many of the Himalayan states, including Gorkha, had traditional institutional arrangements for maintaining militia forces which could be drawn upon in emergencies. The forces were based on settlements on the Mahabharat or Siwalik ranges with "castles" or "fortresses" at suitable places on the hill-tops, and rice-fields in the valleys below. The settlement was known as *thums* and its chief was designated as *umra*. He settled his men there and allotted the rice-fields to them. The men were trained in fighting, and the *umra* was under the obligation of mustering a specified number of fighting men with the prescribed weapons whenever called upon to do so. Most forts in the hill and inner Tarai regions, with the exception of those in such strategic areas as Chisapani and Makwanpur, were under the control of *umras*. It is not possible to hazard an estimate of the size of the militia mobilized through the *umra* system. One can only agree that "they must be pretty numerous."[7]

The *umra* militia was by no means limited to the Himalayan region. Similar systems were followed in other parts of the world in similar situations. For instance, in feudal Europe, "local men of distinction were given hereditary lordship and military command over the country-sides which they dominated and in exchange were expected to maintain fighting men and furnish them at need.[8] The Lord Lieutenants of Tudor England were similarly responsible for "mustering the levies of his country under royal orders for specified and temporary occasions and purposes.[9]

The Gorkhali rulers not only retained the *umra* system but even widened its scope. Immediately after Ran Bahadur's return from India in March 1804, four local men were granted permission to establish a military settlement comprising 101 households of their own as well as of their kinsmen on a tract of land south of the Bagmati river in Makwanpur. Their main duty was to keep ready 100 men armed with bows and poison-tipped and other arrows, as well as guns, increasing the number to 700 within a period of five years. A similar military settlement of 202 households was created in the Hariharpur area of Makwanpur the same day, which provided for 301 fighting men. These two military settlements in Makwanpur thus supported a total of 401 fighting men.[10] This was quite large by the standards of the hill region, where the number of fighting men which the *umra* was obliged to provide was seldom more than twenty.

The *umra* militia was essentially a peasant army, for which military duties were at best a side occupation. For instance, during the wars with Tibet and China (1788-92), "the peasants being generally obliged to repair to the army, agriculture suffered a temporary interruption."[11] Military manpower of this type may have been effective in Gorkha's campaigns against small states in the Himalayan region, but would seem inadequate in the case of Kumaun and other distant territories. It lacked a formal command structure and its actions were not coordinated by centralized discipline. It lacked adequate training. The quality of the weapons it possessed is also suspect, since there is no evidence that the authorities supplied them with any. The *umra* militia may accordingly be described as "a nondescript force of men scarcely trained and indifferently equipped" like their counterparts in Tudor England.[12]

The Gorkhalis retained these militia forces along with the standing army, using their services in Kumaun and elsewhere on the western front. They also used the services of the *umra* for a variety of other functions, such as the mobilization of *jhara* labor for construction of forts, embankments, irrigation canals, and other structures. *Umras* were also responsible for closing unauthorized tracks, manning checkposts, and detaining criminals and other undesirable people who attempted to escape through such tracks.[13]

The Standing Army

The history of the standing Gorkhali army goes back to 1762, when Prithvi Narayan Shah conquered the state of Makwanpur. The booty included at least 700 muskets and large quantities of ammunition. A few months later, the Gorkhalis similarly obtained 500 or 600 muskets and some small pieces of cannon when they defeated an invasion by the forces of the Nawab of Bengal in the Makwanpur area. With those weapons, the Gorkhalis formed at least five companies of troops.[14] This was the nucleus of the standing army of the Gorkhali rulers, which was to strike terror and inspire respect among the rulers of the Himalayan states during the next half-century.

A standing army had several advantages. In the first

place, it could be used in all seasons. There was no longer any need to keep campaigns short so that the men might go back to their fields during the agricultural seasons. Moreover, the use of firearms in the Gorkhali soldier's gear made a standing army indispensable, for such arms were scarce and expensive and their use needed some amount of training. In any case, this innovation showed that fighting was becoming a skilled profession, rather than an occasional enterprise of the peasant-soldier. Indeed, the campaign of territorial expansion in distant territories was hardly possible without a standing professional army.

The standing army of the Gorkhali rulers had a narrow social and territorial base. The subject populations of the Empire were divided into two categories, only one of which was eligible for recruitment. King Prithvi Narayan Shah had instructed his successors to restrict recruitment to four communities, namely, Khas, Magar, Gurung and Thakuri.[15] The list does not mention such other communities as Khawas, Khatri, and Chhetri, who nonetheless gained entry into the standing army in subsequent years. Several ethnic and other communities, collectively described as *praja* were ineligible. They included Rai, Limbu, Kushle, Darai, Kumhale, Danuwar, and Chepang. The Newars of Kathmandu Valley also belonged to that category. The people of both the Tarai region in the south and the Himalayan region in the north were similarly ineligible. It is not clear whether the Gorkhali rulers doubted their loyalty or their martial endowments. The absence of a warrior tradition among these communities must also have weighed in the minds of the rulers. Such a restrictive policy had two negative consequences. Firstly, it reduced the manpower available for military purposes. Secondly, it further alienated the subject populations from their Gorkhali masters.

People belonging to the *praja* communities, even though not eligible for recruitment in the standing army, were given other avenues in which they could contribute to the war efforts. During the Gorkha-Britain war (1814-16), they were mobilized to harass the enemy through tactics which are now regarded as guerrilla tactics. They were permitted to keep the loot, which was listed as "elephants, utensils, cash, and other goods", but were required to hand over arms and ammunition, including muskets, to the government. It is not clear whether these orders were actually carried out. The latest such order dated February 1816, was certainly not obeyed, for the war ended at about the same time.[16] In any case, this was a desperate step taken in a desperate situation and was never repeated.

The Gorkhali standing army was mainly an infantry force, with its organization copied from the Bengal army of the East India Company.[17] The basic unit was the *patti.* Several *pattis* comprised a company. Five companies were often joined together to form a *paltan*, obviously a corrupt form of the English term battalion. A *patti* was headed by a *jamadar*, a company by a *subedar* and a *paltan* by a Captain. A company was usually comprised of 142 officers and men, of whom 26, including the *subedar*, were of officer rank, and 85 soldiers. These 111 officers and men carried weapons, and were collectively designated as *nal*. The remaining 31 men, who were collectively designated as *lajima*, included 17 porters, 9 drummers, and 5 ironsmiths, cobblers, and carpenters. The two categories of *nal* and *lajima* may be designated as combatants and non-combatants or auxiliaries, respectively. Not all companies were of uniform size. There were also companies with as many as 262 men, including the *subedar* and 40 other officers, as well as 174 soldiers and 47 auxiliaries. On one single day in July 1797, King Ran Bahadur issued orders reconfirming the size of 21 companies of whom 17 companies comprised 142 men each, three companies 262 men each, and one as many as 270 men.[18] In Kumaun, royal orders issued in May 1805 provided for a company of 155 men, inclusive of 26 officers, 85 soldiers, and 16 porters. There was also a 12-man artillery unit, since each company was equipped with one piece of cannon.[10]

Chapter 3 (The Administration) had made a reference to the traditional system of *pajani*, under which every *bhardar* and other employee of the Gorkhali Empire was screened every year and reconfirmed, transferred, promoted, or dismissed. The system was applicable to the Gorkhali army as well. But as the Empire grew in size, the Gorkhali rulers at the center delegated their *pajani* authority to the Gorkhali *bhardars* in Kumaun and other provinces. Such delegation was applicable only to the rank and file of the army; the central authorities retained the *pajani* authority over the *bhardars* and military commanders in their own hands. In 1796, King Ran Bahadur Shah promulgated orders providing for security of service to military personnel. He decreed:[20]

> A military employee, once his appointment is confirmed, shall not be dismissed without any reason. Soldiers with a long record of service shall not be dismissed. Even if they are guilty of homicide or any other crime, they may be replaced only with the approval of the government.

In actual practice, the *pajani* system in the provinces, including Kumaun, was used as a system of rotation, particularly in the case of the common soldiers.[21] This meant that a certain number of soldiers were replaced every year by new enlistments. Soldiers who were kept in reserve without pay in this manner were known as *dhakre*.[22] They provided a reserve of military manpower which could be drawn upon in emergencies. This source of military manpower was so important that in Kumaun the local Gorkhali authorities were ordered not to permit *dhakres* to return home without official permission. At the same time, the prospect of reappointment often led many *dhakres* to stay on in Kumaun, rather than go back home.[23]

A Gorkhali company was usually commanded by an officer known as *subedar*, who was appointed, transferred, or dismissed by the central authorities in Kathmandu in the name of the King. Almost all of them belonged to the Gorkhali heartland, with such familiar Gorkhali family names as Khawas, Khatri, Thapa, Baniya, Rana, Khadka, Basnyat, Gurung, Kunwar, and Malla.[24]

The functions and duties of the *subedar* of a Gorkhali company were defined in the letter of appointment. For example, Indra Simha Thapa was appointed as *subedar* of one of the companies stationed in Kumaun with duties as follows:[25]

> Keep your men satisfied. Do not collect unauthorized payments. Do not commit injustice, so that no complaints may reach us. Keep your muskets and other equipment in a state of readiness and remain on alert for war or other assignments according to our orders.

At the time of his appointment, the *subedar* had to sign a bond stipulating the number of *nal* and *lajima* men in his company. He then made the appointments on his own authority, but the provincial Gorkhali *bhardars* had the power to review his selections. *Subedars* were forbidden to keep any *nal* post vacant for any reason. The muster-roll was checked by the Gorkhali *bhardars* in Kumaun and reports were sent to Kathmandu every year.[26]

Deployment of Gorkhali Troops

Companies of the standing army were stationed in the capital, Kathmandu, as well as in different provinces and vassal states. There were two companies each in the eastern provinces of Chainpur, Majhkirat, and Vijayapur.[27] In the western sector, there were nine companies in Palpa, four in Pyuthan, three in Achham, and one in Dullu-Dailekh. The vassal states of Bajhang and Bajura shared a company while Jajarkot accommodated one full company. Jumla had two companies, and Doti as many as eight. Across the Mahakali river, there were 11 companies in Kumaun, 15 in Garhwal, and 38 in the provinces of Kullu, Sirmur, Handur, and Kangra.[28] The number of companies stationed in different provinces and vassal states changed in subsequent years in response to the military activity of the Gorkhali rulers, particularly during the siege of Kangra and the Gorkha-

Britain war. It is difficult to keep track of these changes, but the general trend is clear: the Gorkhali army had an increased presence in Kumaun and other provinces and vassal states after 1805.

Such a wide deployment of the companies of the Gorkhali standing army had the objective of maintaining peace and tranquility in the province and ensuring rapid reinforcements to the army on the front whenever necessary. In particular, it was intended to facilitate the safety of the east-west track and ensure the steady flow of men and material to the front. Yet another objective may have been to awe the local inhabitants, whose loyalty to the Gorkhali rule was always suspect. This was much more so in the case of the vassal states such as Jajarkot, Bajhang, and Bajura, where the emoluments of the Gorkhali troops were paid from resources raised within the vassal states themselves. The Gorkhali military presence there checked the possibility of rebellion and made Gorkhali intervention easy whenever necessary.

Supplementary Forces

As previously noted, about eleven companies of the army were stationed in Kumaun in 1805. At the rate of 101 combatants in each company, including both officers and other ranks, this means a military force of 1,111 combatants. Non-combatants or auxiliaries are excluded from the calculation. A fighting force of about 1,111 men in a relatively large province such as Kumaun cannot certainly be regarded as excessive in a time of war. It is, therefore, hardly surprising that the Gorkhali rulers made supplemental arrangements for meeting emergencies such as foreign invasions. In such eventualities, they granted authority to the provincial authorities to recruit additional troops. Such troops were disbanded once the emergency was over.[79]

For prolonged military campaigns such as the 1789-1791 western campaign, and the post-1804 expansion beyond Kumaun, as well as the wars with Tibet, China and the

British, the Gorkhali rulers supplemented their regular military forces with conscripts from different parts of the Empire as well as from the vassal states. Conscription means the compulsory enlistment of fighting men for military duties. The system, in principle, raised little difficulty in the minds of the subjects of the Gorkhali Empire, for unpaid and compulsory services for meeting the manpower needs of the rulers had a long-established tradition in the states of the Himalayan region in the form of the *jhara* system which was been described in Chapter 2 (Kathmandu and Almora). Even then, coercive methods were often used to round up reluctant conscripts.[30] The system of conscription made it possible for the Gorkhali rulers to increase their military manpower at minimum cost.

Local recruitment was yet another way in which the Gorkhali augmented their military manpower in Kumaun. According to British sources:[31]

> A large number of local people were taken into the Gorkhali army in Kumaun, the percentage in 1814 estimated at about two-thirds. They were not recruited in the regular Gorkhali companies, but were rather considered in the light of a local militia and received regular pay only when on foreign service. They were as a rule under the order of Gorkhali officers; but occasionally were given small commands. The Kumaun levies were armed much in the same way as the regular (Gorkhali) troops, but were inferior to the Gorkhalis in strength, activity and gallantry, though capable, of doing excellent service under leaders.

Desertions

The Gorkhali rulers often faced the problem of desertions from their armed forces. A British source has noted that it was "no uncommon practice among the officers even to throw aside their military garb, and absent themselves without ceremony from their corps, on any temporary disgust they may happen to conceive".[32]

The problem of desertion emerged early in the course of the post-1804 military campaign. In September 1805, Kaji Nayan Simha Thapa a brother of Bhimsen Thapa, who had been deputed to the Kangra front, was instructed to arrest deserters and punish them with amputation of the nose.[33] However, the problem remained intractable and sizeable as the tempo of the Gorkhali military campaign increased in subsequent years. In September 1809, Gorkhali troops sent to Kangra as reinforcements under the command of Kaji Amrit Simha Thapa were ordered:[34]

> Do not desert your company and go over to another company or assignment. If you work hard in your post, I shall give you rewards as recommended by Kaji Amrit Simha Thapa. You will be severely punished if you do not obey his orders. Do not engage in unnecessary quarrels in your company. If anyone does so, I have given orders to punish him according to the seriousness of his offense. You will be severely punished if you tak away your guns and other equipment on the plea of illness or untoward incidents in your family. If you are not satisfied with your assignment, hand over your guns to me. But so long as you remain on duty in Kangra, you must obey the orders of Kaji Amrit Simha Thapa, you obey the orders of Kaji Amrit Simha Thapa with full bravery and loyalty.

This royal order, issued in the name of the King, Girban Yuddha Bikram Shah, is of special interest because of the use of the first person singular. It has few parallels, if any, in the administrative history of the Gorkhali Empire. Accordingly, it seems to be more a personal appeal to the Gorkhali troops sent to Kangra than a formal royal order. Such appeals, however, do not seem to have made any dent on the problem. Two years later, in 1811, Kaji Rewant Kunwar was sent to the Bheri-Sutlej region to arrest armymen who had deserted their posts, failed to join their duties, or mutinied. The scale and seriousness of the problem can be judged from the fact that four companies of Gorkhali troops were placed under his command for the operations.[35] Often the deserters settled down in Kumaun and other occupied territories. The Gorkhali authorities did not encourage such a tendency because of its adverse impact on their military manpower, but were seldom able to take effective counter-measurers. They could only issue orders to deport the settlers, but with the caveat that such action should be taken only if complaints were received from the local people.[36]

Defections to the British side during the Gorkha-Britain war was a more serious and humiliating problem. The scale of the problem can be realized from the fact that the British were able to raise a force of 2,000 irregulars with Gorkhali prisoners during the very first year of the war.[37] By the time the war ended, the British had as many as three battalions formed with Gorkhali defectors. Such defections were started by those who had been recruited within Kumaun itself. According to another British source, during 1815, as the war situation started changing in favour of the British:[38]

> The natives of the (Kumaun) provinces who were employed in the Gorkhali service began to desert in great numbers. Many of them returned to their homes, and more than three hundreds soldiers, including several *sardars* of some importance, joined (the British) and were incorporated in (the British) force."

At times, even troops of the regular Gorkhali army joined the exodus. Many of them belonged to the Gorkhali heartland. One can, therefore, understand why the defectors were described in royal orders as "traitors". There was nothing that the Gorkhali authorities could do either to stem the exodus or to punish the defectors, beyond reallotting the sources of revenue previously allotted to them. They could only confiscate the property of the defectors in the heartland, which they did whenever possible.[39]

Such desertions and defections were not of such a large scale as to harm the overall effectiveness of the Gorkhali standing army in any way. This will be clear when one reviews the successes of the Gorkhali campaign of imperial expansion, particularly during the period from 1786 to 1791. Gorkha's emergence as an imperial power during those years is itself sufficient testimony to the effectiveness of its standing army, which provided the hard core of the Gorkhali military might and formed a part of the Gorkhali establishment committed to the *dhungo* ideology. The other components of the Gorkhali armed forces, namely, conscripts and local levies, lacked this main principle of loyalty to the Gorkhali cause. Moreover, the distinction between the regular troops of the standing army and the conscript troops and local levies is based on the distinction between soldiers and warriors. Warriors fight as the spirit moves them; their actions are not coordinated by centralized discipline. In contrast, soldiers are subordinated to a central command and fight in formation. It has also been said that "warriors defeat others, but it requires soldiers to conquer nations.[40] The question was one of discipline, obedience to command, unity of purpose, and *esprit de corps*.

British sources have generally given a positive evaluation of the capability, bravery, and sense of discipline of the regular Gorkhali troops. Their evaluation is important, since it has come from a side which ultimately defeated the Gorkhalis and reduced the size of their Empire after a bitterly-contested war.

Kirkpatrick has described them as "brave, sufficiently tractable, and capable of sustaining great hardships."[41] According to another British source.[42]

> The regular army of Nepal has been for so long a time accustomed to active service, to a series of constant warfare and victory that the men have become really veteran soldiers, under the advantages of necessary control and a certain degree of discipline; and from their continual successes they have attained a sense of their own value a fearlessness of danger and a contempt of any foe opposed to them. They have much of the true

and high spirit of a soldier that setting life at nought in comparison with the performance of duty and that high sense of honour which forms his most attractive ornament and raises his character to the highest.

Concluding Remarks

In view of such a role of the Gorkhali standing army, the debacle suffered by the Gorkhali state in the 1814-16 war with the British needs an explanation. The debacle did not take place because the army did not do what was expected of it. Indeed, it fought long and hard in the Gorkhali cause. The personal courage and bravery of the Gorkhali armymen won the adulation of the British. They also formed the rationale of arrangements under which they were permitted to recruit Gorkhalis in the British army. The arrangement still continues, albeit in a new form. What then went wrong during 1814-16 ?

The answer to the question is obvious. The army is an important element in the success or failure of any military enterprise, but is nevertheless only one of several elements. Its contribution must be assessed only against the background of the objectives laid down by the political leadership and the adequacy or otherwise of its resources and capacity to attain those objectives. This is where the political leadership of the Gorkhali Empire failed the test, particularly after 1804. I have noted in an earlier volume that the post-1804 campaign of imperial expansion was actually "a series of barren and destructive adventures, culminating in the 1815 debacle.[43] The political leadership bit off more than it could chew. The military strength it was able to mobilize was not adequate to ensure the success of its unrealistic goals. The Gorkhali army certainly cannot be blamed for the mistakes of the political leadership.

NOTES

1. Niccolo Machiavelli, *The Prince and Discourses*, ed. by Max Lerner, 1959, p. 175.

2. Elbridge Colby, "Army" in *Encyclopaedia of the Social Sciences*, 1963, Vol. 2, p. 210.

3. David B. Guralnik (ed.), *Webster's New World Dictionary*, 1972, p. 1388.

4. In August 1814, General Ochterlony wrote to the Governor-General, Lord Hastings: "The Rajas who have been expelled (from the states of the Cis-Sutlej region), did not maintain any or only a very small number of troops, but depended for the defense of their country on the inhabitants themselves." Cited in Ludwig F. Stiller, *The Rise of the House of Gorkha*, 1974, p. 230.

5. Yogi Naraharinath (ed.), *Gorakha Vamshavali* (Genealogy of Gorkha), 1964, pp. 35, 88, 90, 102, and 169.

6. Edwin T. Atkinson, *The Himalayan Districts of the North-Western Provinces*, 1882, Vol. 2, p. 609.

7. Colonel Kirkpatrick, *An Account of the Kingdom of Nepaul*, 1811, pp. 54-55: Mahesh C. Regmi, "The Umra"' *Regmi Research Series*, Year 20, Nos. 6-7, June-July, 1988, pp. 95-98; Separate royal orders of appointment of *umras* in different areas of Nuwakot, Marga sudi 4, 1866 (November 1809), *RRC*, Vol. 40, pp. 147-48; Royal Nepali Army Headquarters, *Nepalako Sainik Itihas* (Military History of Nepal), Kathmandu: The Headquarters, 1992, pp. 83-85. This volume will be cited as RNAH in the notes.

8. Colby (No. 2), p. 210.

9. J.J. Bagley, *Historical Interpretation*, 1971, pp. 52-57.

10. Separate royal orders regarding military settlements in Makwanpur, Chaitra sudi 8, 1860 (March 1804), *RRC*, Vol. 2, pp. 65-68 and 71-74.

11. Kirkpatrick, p. 24.

12. Bagley, p. 52.

13. No. 7 above.

14. Naya Raj Panta, *Shri 5 Prithvinarayanshahako Upadesha* (Teachings of King Prithvi Narayan Shah), p. 327; RNAH, pp. 85-88.

15. RNAH, pp. 161-62.

16. Royal orders to the Khas, Magar, Rai and Limbu inhabitants of Chainpur, Kartik badi 10, 1872 (October 1825), *RRC*, Vol. 42, p. 89; do. to Subba Gambhir Simha Ale and others, Falgun sudi 6, 1872 (February 1816), *RRC*, Vol. 42, p. 224-25.
17. John Pemble, *The Invasion of Nepal*, 1971, p. 26.
18. Royal orders to officers of the Naya Srinath Company, Shrawan sudi 15, 1854 (July 1797), *RRC*, Vol. 25, pp. 516-17; do. to the Khas and other companies, do., pp. 517-26.
19. Instructions to Kaji Ritudhwaj Khawas for Kumaun, Jestha sudi 3, 1862 (May 1805), *RRC*, Vol. 20, pp. 182-85.
20. Royal order to officers and men of Jagir-holding companies, Ashadh sudi 5, 1853 (June 1796), *RRC*, Vol. 20, pp. 48-50; RNAH, pp. 91-92.
21. Stiller, p. 291.
22. Royal order to the Subba of Doti, Aswin sudi 5, 1862 (September 1805), *RRC*, Vol. 6, pp. 531-32.
23. Royal instructions to Subba Gajakesar Pande and Sardar Parashuram Thapa, Ashadh badi 9, 1860 (June 1803), *RRC*, Vol. 20, p. 96.
24. List of *bhardars* and others liable to pay the *Chumawan* levy for the investiture ceremony of King Girban, Poush sudi 13, 1864 (January 1808), *RRC*, Vol. 19, pp. 347-56; Royal order to Sardar Achal Thapa regarding payment of salaries to Subedars and others, Bhadra sudi 15, 1872 (August 1815), *RRC*, Vol. 42., pp. 66-68; Notification in the Mahakali-Sutlej region regarding preparations for the Besahar campaign, Magh sudi 3, 1867 (January 1811), *RRC*, Vol. 38, pp. 715-17.
25. Appointment of Indra Simha Thapa Nagarkoti as *subedar* of the Naya Sabuj Company, Aswin sudi 6, 1862 (September 1805), *RRC*, Vol. 6, pp. 537-38.
26. Royal order to Subedars in the regions west of the Marsyangdi river, Shrawan badi 3, 1855 (July 1798), *RRC*, Vol. 52, pp. 31-32; Instructions to Najiki Bhup Narayan Shahi and others for the Kathmandu-Kangra region, Poush badi 1, 1865 (December 1808), *RRC*, Vol. 36, pp

196-200; Royal order to Subedar Anup Simha Adhikari, Kartik badi 30, 1867 (October 1810), *RRC*, Vol. 38, p. 597; Royal order to *bhardars* in the trans-Bheri region regarding Kaji Rewant Kunwar's assignment, Marga sudi 10, 1868 (November 1811), *RRC*, Vol. 40, p. 317.; Royal order to Chautariya Bam Shah, Bhadra sudi 9, 1872 (August 1815), *RRC*, Vol. 42, p. 61.

27. Appointment of Rambhadra and Chamu Thapa as Subedars in Chainpur, Magh badi 3, 1853 (January 1797), *RRC*, Vol. 25, pp. 341-42; Royal notification to the inhabitants of Majhkirat, Shrawan badi 12, 1850 (July 1793), *RRC*, Vol. 36. pp. 11-12; Appointment of Jayawant Shahi as *Subba* of Majhkirat, Ashadh badi 14, 1856 (June 1799), *RRC*, Vol. 23, pp. 343-44; Instructions to Sardar Bhairav Simha Khawas regarding administration of Vijayapur, Jestha sudi 7, 1865 (May 1808), *RRC*, Vol. 36, pp. 110-11;

28. Royal instructions to Kaji Ritudhwaj Khawas for Kumaun, Jestha sudi 3, 1862 (May 1805), *RRC*, Vol. 20, p. 187; Royal order to the Subedars of Gorkhali troops in Kumaun, Marga badi 1, 1862 (November 1805), *RRC*, Vol. 19, p. 388; Royal order disbanding the Randal Company in Kumaun, Jestha sudi 7, 1865 (May 1808), *RRC*, Vol. 36, pp. 106-7; Royal order to Kaji Rewant Kunwar and others regarding administrative affairs in Garhwal, Bhadra sudi 5, 1867 (August 1810), *RRC*, Vol. 39, pp. 382-89; Royal order to Kaji Amar Simha Thapa in Palpa, Baisakh badi 6, 1862 (April 1805), *RRC*, Vol. 20, p. 138; Royal instructions to Subedar Puran Shahi and others, Jestha badi 12, 1862 (May 1805), *RRC*, Vol. 6, pp. 139-50; *RRS*, Year 15, No. 4, April 1983, pp. 56-60. These instructions cover the provinces of Doti, Bajura, Bajhang, Achham, Dullu-Dailekh and Jajarkot; Royal instructions to Sardars Ranajung and Rudravir for Pyuthan, Shrawan badi 1, 1862 (July 1805), *RRC*, Vol. 6, pp. 192-96; *RRC*, Year 15, No. 4, April 1983, pp. 61-62; Royal order to Surbir Rana and his brothers in Pyuthan, Magh sudi 9, 1855 (January 1798), *RRC*, Vol. 24, pp. 709-11; Royal instructions to Rama Sundar Thapa and Bhajudev Khawas for Jumla, Jestha sudi 14, 1862 (May 1805), *RRC*, Vol. 6, pp. 162-9, *RRS*, do. pp. 60-61. Royal orders to Kajis Ambar Thapa,

and Nayan Thapa for Kangra, Aswin sudi 2, 1862 (September 1805), *RRC*, Vol. 6, pp. 515-16. Similar orders were issued to Gorkhali *bhardars* in Kullu, Sirmur, and Handur also on the same date, do., pp. 510-14.

29. See references to powers of Subbas and other provincial authorities in Kumaun in Chapter 3 (The Administration).

30. Royal orders regarding conscription in Tanahu and other areas in the western hill region, Magh sudi 1, 1862 (January 1806), *RRC*, Vol. 6, pp. 722-23; do., in Salyan, Rukum, Kaski, and other areas, Kartik sudi 9, 1871 (November 1814), *RRC*, Vol. 41, pp. 416-45.

31. Atkinson, p. 624.

32. Kirkpatrick, p. 215.

33. Royal order to Kaji Nayan Simha Thapa and Sardar Indra Simha Thapa, Aswin badi 2, 1862 (September 1805), *RRC*, Vol. 19, pp. 263-64.

34. Royal order to Gorkhali troops sent to Kangra, Aswin sudi 13, 1816 (September 1809), *RRC*, Vol. 40, pp. 105-6.

35. Royal order to Gorkhali armymen and others deputed to the trans-Bheri region, Marga sudi 10, 1868 (November 1811), *RRC*, Vol. 40, p. 317.

36. Royal instructions to Kaji Bahadur Bhandari and Bakshi Dasharath Khatri, Kartik badi 2, 1867 (October 1810), *RRC*, Vol. 39, pp. 449-59.

37. David Bolt, *Gurkhas*, 1967. pp. 59-60.

38. Atkinson, p. 654; Pemble, p. 348.

39. Royal order to Subedar Dharma Raj Khatri, Shrawan badi 11, 1872 (July 1818), *RRC*, Vol. 42, pp. 38; also see pp. 109 and 155-56.

40. Carl J. Couch, *Constructing Civilizations*, 1984, p. 270.

41. Kirkpatrick, p. 215.

42. Atkinson, p. 626; Stiller, p. 291.

43. Regmi, *Kings and Political Leaders*, p. 26.

5

The Revenue System

Just as it is impossible not to taste the honey or the poison that finds itself at the tip of the tongue, so it is impossible for a government servant not to eat up, at least, a bit of the King's revenue. Just as fish moving under water cannot possibly be found out either as drinking or not drinking water, so government servant employed in the government work cannot be found out while taking money for themselves. It is possible to mark the movements of birds flying high up in the sky; but not so is it possible to ascertain the movement of government servants of hidden purpose.

Kautilya[1] *(c 300 B.C.)*

The Gorkhali imperialist policy in Kumaun was basically aimed at securing a territorial base for further expansion. It was not meant to open up new markets for the products of other parts of the Empire, or new sources of materials, or to establish Gorkhali colonies. Rather, the Gorkhalis limited their aim to the raising of resources for the upkeep of the Gorkhali establishment in the province, consisting of Gorkhali administrators and troops. A revenue surplus for appropriation by the center, although a desirable goal, was not a matter of high priority. Indeed, the tax and other revenues that the Gorkhalis were able to mobilize in Kumaun were seldom adequate even to meet the costs of the Gorkhali establishment. This chapter discusses the fiscal policies of the Gorkhali rulers in Kumaun, and the steps they took with the objective of maximizing revenue.

Natural Resources and Economic Activities[2]

The fiscal policies of a state primarily depend on the nature of economic activities. Such activities, in turn, depend on its natural resources which may be discussed under three categories, namely, agricultural lands, forests, and mines. This account is only intended to provide background information for a study of the revenue system in Kumaun, and, therefore, should not be taken as a attempt to describe or to assess the economic potential of the province.

The province of Kumaun was composed of two distinct geographic zones, the Himalayan zone in the north and the monsoon-affected middle and low-attitude zones in the south. The Himalayan zone, "with a mass of tangled peaks and valleys," was covered with snow from October to April. The agricultural season is very short, with wheat or barley as the sole crop, but only in intermittent years. There was thus a chronic shortage of food. Trade with Tibet and handicraft production (woollen blankets, carpets, shawls, etc.) were the main economic activities. In contrast, the southern half of the province is comprised of gently sloping ground, most of it cultivable. The riverain areas are exceptionally fertile, producing rice and other tropical crops. As a result, there was a surplus of food, which was exported to Tibet as well as to the southern plains.

Northern Kumaun and the adjoining areas of western Tibet have been described as "regions of contrasted production," "Western Tibet is very bleak, barren, and inhospitable, and depends entirely on Kumaun for its food supply and other necessities, and its luxuries." On the other hand, Nature has provided it with some very valuable products, "such as wool, medicinal herbs, yak-tails, furs, hides and skins, ponies, goats, sheep, borax, and salt." The contrast in production led to a system of mutual exchange and trade, with the inhabitants of the Himalayan zone as middlemen. As a result, they enjoyed "the highest standard of living" in the province.

At the foot of the hills in the south is a narrow belt full of boulders and gravel, and arid and waterless, but with timber of commercial importance. Cattle were brought there from the southern plains for grazing during the summer months. Elephants caught in these forests were another source of revenue.

The mountain territories of Kumaun produced such metals as copper, lead, iron, and gold although "no mine was of great value." Mines of both copper and iron were operated by individuals under license. Copper was mined in Sira and Gangoli, although in difficult and inaccessible mountainous terrain. Because of the gradual depletion of forests, shortage of charcoal, and difficulties of transportation, costs of production were high. These negative factors were partially compensated for by the high quality compared with imported copper. British sources claim that revenue from copper mines in Kumaun and Garhwal declined after the Gorkhali conquests, "mainly due to the neglect of the Gorkhali government, under which the mines had fallen in and become choked with rubbish."

Imperfect Control

The state's control over these economic resources, particularly agricultural lands, was circumscribed by a number of systems which were traditionally followed not only in Kumaun but throughout the Himalayan region. The most important of these systems was tax-free grants of lands and other sources of income to individuals under the *birta* system, and to religious and charitable institutions under the *guthi* system.[3] The Chand rulers had made both categories of grants on a fairly lavish scale. As a result, their revenue receipts had gone down in the same proportion.

There were also extensive areas of agricultural lands, on which no taxes were paid to the state. This seems to have been the case not only in Kumaun but also in other parts of the western and central areas of the Himalayan region. Such lands belonged for the most part to Brahmins, who seem to have enjoyed the traditional privilege of tax exemption on lands belonging to them or brought under cultivation by them.[4] In practical terms, this meant that no taxes were collected from the homesteads and agricultural lands of Brahmins. It also meant that Brahmins could bring new lands under the plow without any tax liability.

Gorkhali Initiatives

The Gorkhali rulers took several initiatives soon after the conquest to remold the traditional fiscal system in Kumaun and give it a wider base. However, these initiatives seldom yielded the expected benefits.

The first initiative was to reform the system of assessing revenue. The Chand rulers had followed a system which was more or less similar to what later came to be known as the *mahalwari* system in the adjoining British territories. The term *mahal* was there defined as "any local area held under a separate engagement for the payment of the land revenue." This meant that revenue was assessed in a lump sum a year for each district or, at times, a specified area, calculated on the basis of such factors as the nature and level of economic activity, location, and population.[5] The system made it unnecessary to mention specific sources of revenue. The Gorkhalis had planned to replace this system with a new one under which individual households were treated as the basic unit of assessment;[6] but the plan was never implemented.

The second Gorkhali initiative in the fiscal field took the form of widening the fiscal base. The main target was the *birta* owning Brahmin community. The Gorkhalis levied a new one-time tax on *birta* holdings, took over *birta* lands held under titles which they considered invalid, and brought all categories of undeclared lands of Brahmins within the ambit of the fiscal system. The one-time tax on *birta* lands was known as *kusahi bisahi*. The owners were given the choice of surrendering the lands to the state if they were unable or unwilling to pay the tax, or, if cash was not available, making payments in the form of household utensils of copper and brass, as well as gold and silver.[7] In Kumaun, payment was staggered over a period of five or six years, but actually the tax was collected for as many as twelve years.[8] British sources have imputed political motives for its introduction:[9]

> As this tax was very seldom collected, it may be held to have been merely a measure intended to keep the more refractory and intriguing members of that (Brahmin) caste in order. So long as they gave no trouble to the authorities it was not levied, but if the Brahman landholders were suspected of paying more attention to political affairs than to the cultivation of their holding, the tax with arrears was at once demanded."

The conclusion seems basically correct. How else should one take the plea contained in royal orders to the Brahmins "to remain faithful to us, wish our victory, and give blessings to us everyday" ?[10]

The Gorkhali policy was to scrutinize *birta* grants and reconfirm those made by the "legitimate" rulers of Kumaun or their Chief Queens and Crown Princes before 1748, the year when Dip Chand was installed as ruler of Kumaun. Grants made by other individuals, or those which did not specify the boundaries, were confiscated. A similar policy was adopted in respect to undeclared lands held by Brahmins on a tax-free basis. According to the regulations, "In case documentary evidence of title is not available, and in case the local functionaries and landowners, say that they have no knowledge of the land having been granted to any Brahmin by any King, the land shall be confiscated". Confiscation, however, did not mean that the landowners were dispossessed of their lands. Rather, they were usually allowed to keep the lands in their possession on the condition that they paid the prescribed taxes.[11]

Repeated efforts were made to enforce these measures at different levels, provincial, regional and Empire-wide; but large-scale and effective implementation seems to have been absent - indeed, local administrators in Kumaun were instructed even during the final days of the Gorkhali rule in Kumaun to implement the policy. The plan to exploit tax-free *birta* lands as an additional source of revenue thus seems to have had little impact.

The Gorkhalis were careful not to abolish the *birta* system itself, or to change the traditional convention that entitled the state to grant lands and villages to individuals and institutions on a tax-free basis in exercise of its sovereign power. Indeed, the Gorkhalis themselves made several new *birta* grants to local collaborators, as well as new *guthi* endowments. For instance, in 1797 Ran Bahadur granted to his Queen Kantivati all sources of income in the district of Mahriuri in Kumaun, excluding existing *birtas* and *guthis*, for feeding pilgrims and mendicants at a shrine in Garhwal.[12]

Sources of Revenue

The tax system followed in Kumaun under the Gorkhali rule had two main branches. The first was comprised of taxes collected by the provincial authorities and used for financing local expenditures. The second branch was comprised of a number of special one-time levies, as well as an annual tax on civil and military employees. Income from these sources belonged to the royal household in Kathmandu.

(a) The Provincial List

According to British sources, Jog Narayan Malla, the first Gorkhali Subba of Kumaun, had made the first revenue settlement in that province. The chief taxes levied under that settlement were said to be a tax on agricultural lands, a poll tax on each adult male of the population, and a levy from each village to meet the expenses of his own office.[13] The list seems to be incomplete. In 1793, when Nar Shah was appointed Subba of Kumaun, a royal order prescribed the sources from which he was granted authority to collect taxes and other payments. These sources included taxes on agricultural lands and homesteads, duties on trade, income from the sale of river and forest products, mines and mints, interstate property, and fines and penalties collected in the course of the administration of justice.[14] No specific rates were prescribed for these taxes and payments. Since they were traditional sources, the rates must have been fixed by custom, or by what the people could bear.

(b) The Central List

The central list was comprised of a number of one-time taxes and levies, such as a tax on each adult male[15] and a separate levy on village functionaries.[16] Similar one-time levies were imposed during the coronations of Kings Ran Bahadur Shah and Girban.[17] and the sacred thread investiture ceremony of Girban.[18] A special levy was imposed during the wedding of a royal princess in 1803, but it was replaced the following year by another levy meant to repay the debts that Ran Bahadur had incurred during his four years of exile in India.[19] Similar levies were imposed whenever royal charters were issued to local or ethnic communities entitling them to special rights, privileges, or concessions, or reconfirming those they had been enjoying on a customary basis.[20]

Some characteristic features of most of these special levies must also be noted. Firstly, the rates were prescribed by Kathmandu, a practice which was not followed for such taxes as those on agricultural lands and duties on trade . Secondly, those levies were seldom collected by the provincial authorities, the task was usually assigned to men deputed by Kathmandu according to need. Yet another feature was their wide base. The coronation levy, for example, was imposed on all classes of people, from the *subba*, who paid 601 rupees, to those belonging to the *dom*, an untouchable caste, who paid a quarter-rupee for each household. Between these two extremes were government employees, soldiers, local functionaries, landowners, traders and tax farmers. Indeed, no class of people was left untaxed; even a landless peasant paid half a rupee. The *darshan-bhet*, in contrast, was a perennial source of free-floating resources. The tax was collected from every employee, both civil and military, on his initial appointment, as well as promotion or confirmation during the annual *pajani*.[21] Income from these levies, although officially meant for specific purposes, were often used in Kumaun and elsewhere for urgent military purposes. For instance, in 1803, a sum of 3,000 rupees from revenue collected through the coronation levy was appropriated for paying the salaries of Gorkhali troops in Jumla.[22]

Two Stages: The Ijara System[23]

Two stages in the development of the fiscal system in Kumaun can be easily distinguished, corresponding to the stages in the development of the system of general administration described in Chapter 3. During the first stage (1791-1804), when Kumaun was a separate administrative unit, the administrator, or *subba*, was the kingpin of the fiscal administration, with broad powers of assessment, collection, and disbursement of revenue. The second stage began in 1805, when the post of provincial *subba* became defunct. The function of assessment was then taken over by the regional authorities. Settlements were made with representatives of the local community and periodically revised with Kathmandu's approval under a system which was known as *thekbandi*.

During the first stage, the *subba* collected revenue under the *ijara* system. The term is of Arabic origin, which, in India, denoted a farm or lease of the revenue of a village or district. Under that system, the Gorkhalis assigned their fiscal authority in a specified area, or in respect to a specified source of revenue, to an individual for a specific period for payment of an amount stipulated in advance. The *ijaradar*, consequently, did not have to declare what he collected, anything above the stipulated amount was his own profit, and anything below was his loss. The alternative was the *amanat* system, under which revenue was collected by salaried employees and any profit or loss belonged to the central government. The *amanat* system made it possible for the Gorkhalis to receive the entire amount actually collected, but entailed costs of collection and risks of inefficiency and corruption, whereas the *ijara* system guaranteed a regular amount of revenue. Almost all the Gorkhali *subbas* in Kumaun exercised their fiscal authority in the capacity of *ijaradars*. Nar Shah (1792-94) was the only exemption, but his *amanat* status was modified by a provision entitling him to appropriate a commission of 6.25 percent of revenue actually collected, in addition to his official emoluments.

Under the *ijara* systems, the *subba* collected revenue from sources authorized by the central authorities (and also from sources not so authorized), made the prescribed disbursements, paid a stipulated sum ranging between 12,000 and 14,000 rupees to the central account, and appropriated for himself the surplus, if any. But the *ijara* payment did not reach the central treasury in Kathmandu. The reason was that a number of provincial expenses were met from this source. These expenses included the salaries of local military recruits, compensation for new tax-free *birta* land grants and *guthi* endowments, and expenses of elephant-hunts.

The *ijara* system suffered from two main defects, Firstly, it prevented the Gorkhalis from garnering a revenue surplus from the province. Secondly, it kept down the number of troops which could be financed through the provincial revenues. Indeed, the number of troops had reached a state of stasis as the *subba-ijaradar* assumed obligation for the salaries and other benefits of only about 11 companies. The cost of reinforcements, if any, was paid from the central account.

The Second Stage: The Thekbandi System

In 1805, the Gorkhali rulers abolished the *ijara* system of revenue collection and disbursement in Kumaun, and switched over to the *thekbandi* system. Settlements continued to be made with representatives of the local community, but they made payments directly to the Gorkhali companies and others to whom the revenue had been assigned as emoluments. The role of the provincial authorities was limited to periodic reviews of assessments and assignations. They were no longer responsible for collection and disbursement. The procedure of finalizing the new arrangements was as follows:[24]

> Ascertain the sources of revenue and their yield during the rule of the Chands, and the changes that were made after our conquest. Prescribe new schedules in such a manner that the amount of revenue does not decline and the people feel satisfied. Have the local people and revenue functionaries affix their signatures on these schedules, and submit a copy to us for our approval.

In 1810, the Bhandari-Khatri team was similarly instructed:[25]

> Make necessary arrangements to insure that the amount of revenue does not decline, armymen do not complain, and the territory becomes prosperous. Also insure that the arrangements made by you remain effective for a long time and you get credit, rather than blame. If necessary, give some concessions to the people.

Revenue settlements under the *thekbandi* system were made with a prominent local person whose duties were as follows:[26]

> Do not harass or oppress the inhabitants of the area under your jurisdiction, so that no complaints may reach us. Promote land reclamation and settlement, and disburse the amounts stipulated under the *thekbandi* arrangements to military personnel according to orders issued by the provincial authorities.

The *thekbandi* settlements made in Kumaun by the Gorkhalis were thus nothing more than adjustments in the amount of payments dating back to Chand times, irrespective of the system of collection, *ijara* or *amanat*.[27]

The settlements were marked by bargaining. For example, in 1805, the revenue assessment in the district of

Phaldakot in Kumaun was fixed at 7,000 rupees. The figure was reduced to 6,169 rupees because sources yielding 831 rupees were assigned for other purposes. Subsequently, the figure was raised by 2,500 rupees to finance the salaries of newly recruited troops, the total amount being 8,669 rupees. The troops were later disbanded, but the assessment was not restored to the previous figure. In 1810, when the local people complained, the central authorities reduced the amount to 7,384 rupees.[28] Revenue assessment in the district of Phaldakot thus increased from 7,000 rupees to 7,384 rupees during the 6-year period from 1805 to 1810, that is, by about 5.5 percent. This can by no means be regarded as excessive.

However, this was not a typical case. In the Himalayan district of Darma, the assessment increased by 50 percent from 5,000 rupees in 1791 to 7,501 rupees in 1812.[29] In that district, as well as in the other Himalayan districts of Juhar and Byas, the incidence of taxation was also increased indirectly by providing that a stipulated portion of the assessed figure be paid in commodities.[30] No information is available about the nature of the commodities supplied by the people of these districts in fulfilment of their fiscal obligations, or about the rates at which cash assessments were converted into commodities. But it can be said with certainty that they were unfavourable for the tax-payers. How else can one explain why the people of Juhar in 1813 were allowed a reduction in the percentage of revenue payable in the form of commodities from 50 to 25 as a concession ?[31]

Unauthorized Collections

The revenue assessments mentioned above during both periods of Kumaun's fiscal history are only official figures. The provincial and other authorities actually collected more, both through higher rates of existing taxes and new impositions. From 1791 to 1805, the peasants were squeezed by the *subba-ijaradar* of the province. A British source has noted that the *subba*, of every Gorkhali province, and "every man in authority under him, takes from his inferiors as much as he can."[32] The rates of taxes and other payments that the *subba-ijaradar* was empowered to collect were seldom specified. He was only told to do so as during the term of his predecessor. That is to say, collections were made on the basis of precedent or custom. But since precedent or custom are rather nebulous factors, the *subba* possessed a wide degree of discretion.

Against this background, the distinction between so-called regular and unauthorized collections was not very clear. Any new payment collected by the *subba*, or any enhancement in the rates of current payments, could be ignored if it was not high enough to prompt the local inhabitants to vote with their feet or send delegations to argue their case before the central authorities in Kathmandu. Within those limits, the *subba* was free to do almost whatever he liked for maximizing his income. Indeed, the *subba* wielded so much power that in one case he increased the revenue assessment figure by one-fourth at one stroke. This happened in 1800, when Subba Dhaukal Basnyat replaced the 16-*anna* rupee used as a unit of account in revenue collection by a 20-anna rupee. Since both were fictional units, no one-rupee coin being in actual circulations, this meant that the tax-payer had to pay 20 *annas* against 16 *annas*, previously, thereby "impoverishing" him. The decree was cancelled by the central authorities the following year, but the excess amount was not refunded to the tax-payers.[33]

The Gorkhali rulers were unable to check the collection of such illegal payments, but only issued exhortations, which remained inoperative. One such exhortation, addressed to Subba Gajakesari Pande in July 1803, is given below:[34]

> We have received reports that the *subbas* of Kumaun have been collecting payments that have not been officially sanctioned, or assessed on any specific source. Such an evil practice is not followed anywhere in our territories. The collection of unauthorized payments from the people is a sin.

Such practices, however, were natural given the wide powers of the *subba*. During the period when collection and disbursement of revenue were the responsibility of the *subba-ijaradar*, the central authorities had no knowledge of actual collections. King Ran Bahadur and his successors made repeated efforts to collect such information, but did not succeed.[35]

The situation did not improve even after the introduction of the *thekbandi* system. Sources of revenue were then assigned to Gorkhali companies and it was the company's agents who collected illegal payments in various forms and often even from sources which had not been assigned to them.[36] A British source has recorded:[37]

> On the completion of the survey a detailed account of each pargunna, showing the numbers, names, size, and extent of the villages, was submitted for the approbation of the court of Nepal. The demand thus authorized, was by no means excessive or unreasonable but the absence of a controlling power on the spot, rendered the arrangements almost nugatory and the military chiefs were enabled to evade it by the power vested in them of imposing fines at their own discretion.

The situation worsened progressively in subsequent years. In 1810, the Bhandari-Khatri team was ordered to submit reports, countersigned by prominent local persons, on unauthorized exactions by the local authorities. It was also ordered to interrogate them in the presence of the complaints, obtain confessions, realize the excess amount paid, and punish the guilty persons.[38] In 1813 a delegation from Kumaun visited Kathmandu with the complaint that in addition to *thekbandi* payments, they were being forced to provide free supplies of rice and vegetables every day. A similar delegation from Darma complained that the *thekbandi* holder "demands additional payments and tortures us if we refuse to pay".[39] All this, however, was a mere cry in the wilderness of Gorkhali rule in Kumaun.

Concluding Remarks

The Gorkhali rulers failed to adopt an equitable and effective system of revenue assessment during their quarter-century-long occupation of Kumaun. Ultimately, they found no alternative but to continue the system followed by their Chand predecessors, although at somewhat higher levels of assessment. (But the official assessment figures represented only the tip of the iceberg, for the provincial authorities actually collected much more through higher rates and extra impositions.) The Gorkhali revenue system in Kumaun accordingly fattened the provincial authorities and their local agents at the cost of both the people and the central government. To be sure, the Gorkhali rulers believed in the principle that "the money of the people must either remain with them or be paid to us; it cannot be appropriated by cunning people"[40], but they never succeeded in implementing that principle effectively in Kumaun.

NOTES

1. Cited in D. Mackenzie Brown; *The White Umbrella: Indian Political Thought from Manu to Gandhi*, 1964, p. 58.
2. This section is based on the following sources: Edwin T. Atkinson, *The Himalayan Districts of the North-western Provinces of India*, 1882; S.D. Pant, *The Social Economy of the Himalayans*, 1935; Jagadish Chandra and Manish Kumar Raha, "*Divergent Trends of Transformation of the Kumaun Bhutiya*," in Christoph Von Furer-Haimendorf, *Asian Highland Societies*, 1981; Ram Chand Guha, *The Unquiet Woods*, 1989.
3. A detailed exposition of these systems is contained in Mahesh C. Regmi, *Land Tenure and Taxation in Nepal*, Vol. 2 (1965) and Vol. 4 (1968).
4. Pillar inscription of King Prithvi Malla of Dullu, Shaka Year 1279/1367 A.D., in Yogi Naraharinath, *Itihas Prakasha* (Light on history), 2013 (1956), Vol. 2, pt. 1, pp. 58-67; Surya Mani Adhikari, *Paschima Nepalako Aitihasika Anweshana* (Historical exploration of western Nepal), 2043 (1986), pp. 8-10.

5. B.H. Baden Powell, *The Land System of British India*, 1979 (reprint), Vol. II, p. 30.
6. Royal instructions to Subba Nar Shah of Kumaun, Poush sudi 13, 1849 (January 1793); *RRC*, Vol. 5, pp. 234-39, *RRS*, Year 4, No. 9, September 1, 1972, pp. 171-72; Royal order to Kitigwal Budha regarding revenue assessment in Darma, Chaitra sudi 5, 1868 (March 1812), *RRC*, Vol. 40, pp. 410-11. A similar royal order for Juhar was issued on Falgun badi 4, 1867 (February 1811), *RRC*, Vol. 38, pp. 734-36.
7. *Regmi Research Series*, Year 4, No. 9, September 1, 1972, pp. 173-74.
8. Royal order to the Brahmin *birta* owners of Kumaun, Ashadh badi 9, 1860 (June 1803), *RRC*, Vol. 20, p. 87.
9. Atkinson, p. 614.
10. No. 8 above.
11. Royal instructions to every Gorkhali *bhardar* deputed to Kumaun mention these policies with minor variations. See in particular "Royal instructions to Kaji Ritudhwaj Khawas for Kumaun, Jestha sudi 3, 1862 (May 1805), *RRC*, Vol. 5, pp. 526-35; Royal order to Dittha Jagdeo Thapa for Garhwal, Poush badi 4, 1869 (December 1812), *RRC*, Vol. 41, pp. 181-82; Atkinson, p. 614.
12. Birta grant to Padmanidhi Upreti in Kumaun, Kartik sudi 11, 1867 (November 1810), *RRC*, Vol. 38, p. 604; Royal order by King Ran Bahadur and Kantavati Devi regarding endoment of revenues from the district of Mahriuri in Kumaun for the Shrine of Kedarnath in Garhwal, 1854 (1797), *RRC*, Vol. 37, pp. 123-24.
13. Atkinson, p. 612.
14. See No. 6 above.
15. Royal notification to the people of Kumaun, Ashadh badi 13, 1866 (June 1809), *RRC*, Vol. 40, pp. 65-66.
16. Royal order to the *Kamins, Sayanas*, etc. of Kumaun, Ashadh badi 9, 1860 (June 1803), *RRC*, Vol. 5, p. 383.
17. "The Gadimubarakh Levy", in *RRS*, Year 20, No. 2,

February 1988, pp. 21-24; Royal order to Subedar Rudravir Shah and others regarding *Gadimubarakh* levy in Kumaun, Ashadh badi 13, 1853 (June 1796), *RRC*, Vol. 23, p. 92; Imposition of *Gadimubarakh* levy in Kumaun, Ashadh badi 13, 1853 (June 1796), *RRC*, Vol. 23, p. 88-91.

18. See No. 5 above; Royal order to the people of Kumaun, Shrawan sudi 12, 1868 (July 1811), *RRC*, Vol. 40, p. 251.
19. "Ran Bahadur Shah's Expenses in Banaras", *RRS*, Year 20, No. 3, March 1988, pp. 31-37; Collection of *salami* levy in Garhwal, Chaitra badi 8, 1863 (March 1807), *RRC*, Vol. 5, pp. 151-54.
20. Royal order to Chautariya Bam Shah, Baisakh badi 2, 1853 (April 1796), *RRC*, Vol. 19, p. 104.
21. "The *Darshan-Bhet* Levy," *RRS*, Year 20, No. 6-7, June-July 1988, pp. 86-91.
22. Royal order to Bhupal Shahi and others, Ashadh badi 9, 1860 (June 1803), *RRC*, Vol. 20, p. 88.
23. This section is based on royal instruction to the *subbas* of Kumaun which have already been cited in Chapter 3 (The Administration).
24. Royal instructions to Kaji Ritidhwaj Khawas for Kumaun, Jestha sudi 3, 1862 (May 1805), *RRC*, Vol. 5, pp. 520-35.
25. Royal instructions to Kaji Bahadur Bhandari and Bakshi Dasharath Khatri, Kartik badi 2, 1867 (October 1810), *RRC*, Vol. 39, pp. 449-59.
26. Royal order to Kitigwal Budha, 1812. (See No. 6.)
27. do.
28. Royal order to Chautariya Bam Shah as Kaji Rewant Kunwar regarding revenue assessments in Phaldakot, Marga sudi 4, 1867 (November 1810), *RRC*, Vol. 38, pp. 655-57.
29. See No. 26 above also: Mahesh Raj Pant, "Vira Bhakti Thapa", *Purnima*, Year 3, No. 4, Magh 1, 2023 (January 14, 1967), p. 57; Royal order to Chautariya Bam Shah and Subba Hastadal Shah, Marga sudi 4, 1867 (November 1810), *RRC*, Vol. 38, pp. 648-49; do. to Radhapati Pande, do., pp. 649-52.

30. do.

31. Royal order to Bijaya Simha Budha, Chaitra sudi 1, 1869 (April 1813), *RRC*, Vol. 39, p. 579.

32. Francis Hamilton, *An Account of the Kingdom of Nepal*, 1819 (reprint 1971), p. 105.

33. Royal instructions to Subba Rudrabir Shah, Shrawan sadi 8, 1859 (July 1802), *RRC*, Vol. 24, pp. 571-85.

34. Royal order to Kaji Gajakesari Pande, Ashadh badi 9, 1860 (June 1803), *RRC*, Vol. 20, p. 94.

35. Royal order to Amar Simha, Bakheti, and others for scrutiny of records of revenue collection in Kumaun, Marga sudi 11, 1852 (November 1795), *RRC*, Vol. 9, p. 17, do. to local functionaries in Kumaun, do. The order accused them of having embizzled a sum of 18,000 rupees. It is not clear how Ran Bahadur calculated the figure; Royal order to Chautariya Bam Shah regarding scrutiny of accounts of revenue collections made by Subba Prabal Rana in Kumaun, Chaitra sudi 15, 1853 (April 1797), *RRC*, Vol. 25, p. 339. The problem was Empire-wide, as a royal order to Dataram Bhatta and Ranbir Thapa in July 1862 (Shrawan badi 8, 1862) shows, *RRC*, Vol. 6, pp. 115-16; Royal order to Rajas, landowners, etc. in the Bheri-Garhwal region, Poush sudi 2, 1868 (December, 1812), *RRC*, Vol. 40, p. 328.

36. Royal order to Gorkhali companies in Kali-Kumaun, Falgun badi 12. 1868 (February 1813), *RRC*, Vol. 39, pp. 523-24.

37. G. W. Traill, "Statistical Sketch of Kumaun", *Asiatic Researches*, XVI (1829), p. 190, cited in L.F. Stiller, *The Rise of the House of Gorkha*, 1975, p. 267.

38. Royal instructions to Kaji Bahadur Bhandari and Bakshi Dasharath Khatri, Kartik badi 2, 1867, (October 1810), *RRC*, Vol. 39, p. 455.

39. Royal order to the *Fouzdars*, *Kamins* etc. of Sor district in Kumaun, Marga sudi 1, 1870 (November 1813), *RRC*, Vol. 41, p. 386; do. to Chautariya Bam Shah for Darma, Baisakh sudi 3, 1870 (April 1813), *RRC*, Vol. 41, pp. 258-59, do to agents of Gorkhali companies in Darma and Byas,

Baisakh sudi 3, 1870 (April 1813), *RRC*, Vol. 41, pp. 257-58; Royal order to agents of companies with *jagir* assignations in Kali-Kumaun, Falgun badi 12, 1869 (February 1813), *RRC*, Vol. 39, p. 523.

40. Royal order to Baijanath Giri and Tula Shahi in Rukum, Jestha sudi 3, 1864 (May 1807), *RRC*, Vol. 20, p. 342; Public notification for the three cities of Kathmandu Valley, Poush sudi 15, 1838 (December 1781), *RRC*, Vol. 5, pp. 627-628.

6

The Jagir System

Homesteads and rice-fields should be provided to the soldiers that the King needs. They will then apply water and manure on their lands and appropriate the shares of both tiller and landlord. This will make them free of care about their families and keep their chests strong, whether at the palace or in the provinces. Do not let bhardars and armymen amass wealth. give them only honors according to their qualifications. Wealthy persons cannot wield the sword and kill the enemy or be killed themselves. My sword will resound in all the four directions if bhardars and armymen do not live a life of luxury.

King Prithvi Narayan Shah[1]

This Chapter seeks to answer the following questions: How were the Gorkhali *bhardars* and armymen, the twin pillars of Gorkhali imperial rule in Kumaun, paid for their services? What were the institutional arrangements that the Gorkhali authorities introduced in Kumaun for that purpose ? How did the province bear the burden ? How did the Gorkhali *bhardars* and armymen fare under these arrangements ? I shall limit the discussion to the regular emoluments of *bhardars* and the standing army; Gorkhalis who were employed in Kumaun on an *ad hoc* basis, such as a militia, conscript troops, and local levies, were not provided with regular emoluments, and, therefore, are not included in this discussion. The emoluments of administrative personnel deputed to Kumaun on short-term or specific duties will similarly be omitted. They were all *ad hoc* payments from *ad hoc* sources outside the ambit of the regular Gorkhali fiscal system.

Categories of Regular Emoluments

The Gorkhali rulers paid emoluments on a regular basis to their employees according to two methods. The first method was payments in cash from the central or provincial treasury. A company of the standing army which received its emoluments in cash on a monthly basis was known as *darmahadar*. The second method was the assignation of specific sources of income, where collection was the responsibility of the assignee, not of the government. Such assignations were known as *jagir*, a term of Persian origin, which, in Mughal India, denoted a form of tenure "in which the public revenues of a given tract of land were made over to a servant of the state, together with the powers requisite to enable him to collect such revenue."[2]

The Gorkhali rulers preferred *jagir* assignations to payments in cash from the state or provincial treasury. Regulations issued in early 1793 for the Gorkhali Empire prescribed that *bhardars* and armymen should be paid emoluments in cash only if sources of income were not available for *jagir* assignations.[3] Provincial authorities in Kumaun were similarly instructed to pay the salaries of Gorkhali armymen in cash only if they did not accept *jagir* assignations.[4] The reasons for such preference for *jagir* assignations are easy to explain. The Gorkhalis had never had an abundance of revenue in cash. They also lacked systematic collecting and accounting systems. The *jagir* system not only solved such problems, but also saved them the trouble of collection and disbursement of revenues.[5] For the employee, on the other hand, cash salaries were more convenient, because *jagir* involved the risks and problems of collection and, therefore, the incomes were uncertain. The provincial authorities were willing to pay cash salaries, but money was always in short supply. Among the eleven companies of the standing army stationed in Kumaun, seven were paid emoluments in cash.[6] A *darmahadar* company's salary bill amounted to 750 rupees a month, or 9,000 rupees a year, with the *subedar* getting 30 rupees and a soldier 5 rupees a month.[7] All these *darmahadar* companies were converted to *jagir*-holding after the introduction of the *thekbandi* system of revenue collection in 1805.[8]

Jagir Schedules

In the Gorkhali Empire, *jagir* assignations usually had two components, namely, *khet* and *khuwa*. The term *khet* means rice-field, but was also used to denote 100 *muris* (approximately 1.25 hectares) of rice-lands. *Khuwa* meant money incomes from homestead and other taxes. Top-ranking officers received both, while others were entitled only to *khet* lands.

The Gorkhali rulers prescribed standard schedules of *jagir* assignations for both their *bhardars* and the standing army. A *chautariya's jagir* was comprised of 125 *khets* of rice-fields, and a *khuwa* income of 4001 rupees. The figures were 116 *khets* of rice-fields and 3,500 rupees for a *kaji*, and 80 *khets* and 1,600 rupees for a *sardar*. The *jagir* assignations of *bhardars* not only provided them with emoluments and perquisites, but also carried a number of obligations. A *sardar* was required to keep 22 fighting men trained in the use of muskets, and to employ the inhabitants of his *khuwa* for the transportation of military supplies. The figures were 45 musketmen for a *kaji* and 46 for a *chautariya*. Each of these *bhardars* was also required to maintain one piece of cannon.[10]

In the standing army, the *subedar's jagir* was comprised of 11 *khets* of rice-fields and a *khuwa* income of 400 rupees. The other ranks received only *khets*, a soldier getting 2 *khets*. Personnel of the lowest ranks, such as porters, received only 1.6 *khets* each. The *jagir* of one company totalled 317.60 *khets* in the heartland areas, and 338.50 *khets* in Kumaun. The difference was due to the fact that a Kumaun company included an artillery unit. Provision was made for a *khuwa* income of 695 rupees in both cases.[11]

A Unit of Account

The *jagir* schedules for both *bhardars* and armymen mentioned above give the impression that the system was quite simple and limited to the assignation of rice-fields and homesteads. But this was by no means the case. The system acquired a complex form for the reason that rice-fields and homesteads were often not readily available for assignation. Consequently, not all *bhardars* and armymen who were assigned income from such sources could actually receive them.

The Gorkhali rulers resolved the problem in an ingenious manner. Shortage of rice-fields and homesteads did not deter them from listing these sources in *jagir* assignations. But when no lands and homesteads were actually available, they commuted the assignation into a cash payment at a standard rate of 25 rupees a *khet*. Shortfalls, if any, were met through assignations of revenue from other sources, or through *ad hoc* disbursements. In other words, the *khet* mentioned in *jagir* assignations was only a unit of account, rather than actual rice-fields.

Official Value of Jagir Assignations

At the official conversion rate of 25 rupees a *khet*, a chautariya's *jagir* of 125 khets yielded 3,125 rupees, with a *khuwa* income of 4,001 rupees a year, totalling 7,126 rupees. Similarly, a *kaji's jagir* of 116 khets and a *khuwa* income of 3,500 rupees, yielded a total income of 6,400 rupees. The figure was 3,600 rupees in the case of a *sardar* for 80 *khets* and a *khuwa* income of 1,600 rupees.

The following table gives the official value of the annual *jagir* assignations of select officers and men of a Company.

The 338.80 *khets* comprising the *jagir* of a Gorkhali Company in Kumaun accordingly yielded 8470 ruppes at the rate of 25 rupees a *khet*. The *khuwa* income of 695 rupees brought up the total amount to 9,165 rupees. In the heartland areas, the figures were 7.940 rupees for 317.60 *khets*, and a *khuwa* income of 695 rupees, making a total amount of 8,635 rupees for a 142-man company.[12]

Table

Official Value of Jagir Schedules for Gorkhali Troops

Designation	*Khet*	*Official Value (Rs.)*	*Khuwa (Rs.)*	*Total (Rs.)*
Subedar	11	275	400	675
Jamadar	6	150	55	205
Adjutant, Major, Kote	4	100	25	125
Soldier	2	50	x	50

The Gap

The official value of *jagir* assignations does not reflect the actual position; for there was usually a gap between the official value and the amount that the assignee was actually able to collect. The reasons are many. They include difficulties of collection, the distance between the place where the *jagir* assignee was posted and the region where the sources of income was located, tenurial diversities, and natural disasters.

(1) Problems of Collection

Collection of taxes and other payments from peasant communities has been a difficult task in almost all parts of the world throughout history, and the Gorkhali experience was no exception. In Kumaun, difficulties of collection mainly stemmed from the unruly and recalcitrant attitude of tax-payers, particularly in the Himalayan districts of Juhar, Darma and Byas. Chapter 1 (The Gorkhali Empire) has noted that these remote districts were brought under Gorkhali control only in 1795. Even then, the local people persisted in their defiant attitude and continued to "hold up payments and assassinate tax collectors."[13]

The Gorkhali authorities devised an ingenious way to solve the problem of delay or default. They spread *jagir* assignations over several districts, thus widening and minimizing the risk-base. The district of Juhar, for example, paid *thekbandi* revenue amounting to 6,000 rupees in cash, and commodities worth 2,000 rupees. Of the cash payment, a sum of 4,934 rupees was assigned to five Gorkhali companies. Three of those companies were assigned a sum of 983 rupees each, while the other two were assigned 1,250 rupees and 833 rupees respectively. Similarly, Darma and Byas paid a total amount of 10,401 rupees, including 3,000 rupees in commodities, but as many as 11 companies had been assigned *jagirs* in those districts, amounting on average (in cash only) to 672 rupees for each company. Since the salary bill of a Gorkhali company of standard size amounted to 9,165 rupees, these assignations represented only part payments.[14]

(2) *The Problem of Distance*

The Gorkhali *bhardars* in Kumaun were seldom granted *jagir* within the province itself. Their *jagirs* were mostly located in the heartland territories of the Empire. For example, Subba Nar Shah thus owned a *jagir* in Lamjung.[15] The situation became more complicated as *bhardars* of higher ranks and influence were posted in Kumaun and other territories in the west after 1804. *Jagir* assignations were then made to them in widely dispersed parts of the Empire. For example, in 1810, Kaji Ambar Simha Thapa, who was commanding the Gorkhali army in the Sutlej region, was granted sources of income in the heartland areas of Kathmandu Valley and the adjoining hill regions, (including Dolakha and Jhangajholi in the east, and Nuwakot and Gorkha in the west), as well as in the Tarai provinces of Bara, Saptari, and Mahottari).[16] Several companies of the standing army, although posted in Kumaun and elsewhere on the western front, similarly held *jagirs* in the heartland areas. It is not possible to ascertain the number of such companies, but it seems to have been fairly large.[17]

The location of the *jagirs* of *bhardars* and companies of the standing army outside Kumaun had an impact on both the Gorkhali state and the *jagir* beneficiaries. For the state, it meant that the Gorkhali authorities subsidized the cost of their provincial administration through resources in the Gorkhali heartland. In other words, the province, while contributing little to the state treasury in Kathmandu, absorbed the resources of other areas in the Gorkhali Empire. For the *jagir* beneficiaries, it gave rise to difficulties in collecting payments from source dispersed over different parts of the Empire. There was no guarantee that they could receive their *jagir* incomes on a regular basis to meet their living expenses at the places where they were posted.

(3) Impact of Tenurial Diversities

The question was not of distance alone between the place where the *jagirdar* was posted and the place where his *jagir* was located. Of greater importance were differences in systems of land tenure and taxation in different parts of the Empire. In the present context, it will be sufficient to describe these systems in two regions, the regions west of the Bheri river, and the heartland areas, including Kathmandu Valley. The difference may be briefly explained as follows: In the trans-Bheri region, land itself was not granted, but only the income, which was usually in cash. In contrast, in the heartland areas, *jagir* meant actual possession and control of rice-fields. Kirkpatrick had the heartland areas in mind in his description of the methods followed by the Gorkhali rulers for the payment of emoluments to armymen. He writes:[18]

> The most usual mode, and the one most agreeable to the troops, is that of putting them in possession of (rice-fields) on which they very commonly settle their families, whom they can maintain much better in this manner, than by the pecuniary stipend to which they would be otherwise entitled.

Kirkpatrick also noted that the *jagirdar* "generally satisfies himself with cultivating a few moories, in which he raises fruit or vegetables, leaving the rest to the Mohi, or undertaker, with whom he engages."

The Gorkhali authorities in Kathmandu, however, often ignored the tenurial diversities between Kumaun and the heartland areas. A few weeks after Kirkpatrick's visit, the Regent, Bahadur Shah, issued an order specifying the rights of a government employee who was dismissed during the annual *pajani* and was accordingly dispossessed of his *jagir*.[19] The arrangements envision a situation in which actual possession of residential structures and agricultural lands was vested in the *jagir*-holder, who appointed the tenants himself and shared the produce equally. Three years later, in June 1796, King Ran Bahadur, in a proclamation to companies of the standing army, decreed:[20]

> Assign available rice-fields according to the prescribed schedules in an equitable manner. In case actual receipts of cash payments, paddy, or wheat exceed the figures mentioned in the schedule, the surplus shall be deposited at the central treasury. In case the lands are damaged by floods or wash-outs, we shall determine the amount of loss and meet the shortfall, except when the *jagir* assignee leaves the lands uncultivated. In case he is dismissed from service without any charge, he shall be entitled to his share of the wheat crop.

These arrangements may have been appropriate for the heartland areas but they were actually decreed for the entire Gorkhali Empire, including Kumaun. Accordingly, they were unenforceable and remained unenforced in Kumaun and other provinces.

The following example shows how *jagir* assignations held by Gorkhali troops in Kumaun actually operated in the heartland areas, and affected the village society and economy. In May 1808, one company of troops in Kumaun was placed under the command of Chautariya Bam Shah, with rice-fields in Tanahu in the western hill region as *jagir*. The fields were tilled by tenants, some of whom lived in other villages, the central authorities cancelled the allotments of outsiders, and ordered that the fields be divided among local families who possessed inadequate plots or were landless, according to the size of the family. The tenant was ordered to pay rents to the *jagir*-holders designated by the Company, as well as to other customary payments. He was also ordered to provide loans and advances up to the total value of the rent. Tenants who did not obey the orders of the *jagir*-holder, or kept the fields uncultivated, were threatened with eviction. It is possible that the ban on outsiders was aimed more at making it easy for the authorities to round up recalcitrant and defaulting tenants than at protecting the interests of the local inhabitants.[21]

The system of crop-sharing on *jagir* rice-fields in the heartland areas suffered from many defects from the viewpoint of the assignee. The main defect was that his *jagir* income was indeterminate. It consisted of a share in the actual output which naturally fluctuated from year to year. It was the first charge on the output, but varied with the yield. There was also little that the *jagirdar* could do if the tenant cheated in the sharing or cultivated the land negligently, or even did not do so at all. Cultivators were ordered to harvest and thresh the crop in the presence of the *jagir* assignee and local functionaries, but this was seldom possible. Because of these problems, the Gorkhali rulers gradually introduced a new system under which rents were fixed at a level determined by the potential yield, rather than by the actual yield. A system of proportional rents was thus changed to a fixed-rent system.[22]

Notwithstanding such a reform in the method of assessment, *jagir* rents continued to be assessed in kind, but cultivators were permitted to pay their rents in money at current market prices.[23] This arrangement was possible only in an exchange economy which did not exist in most parts of the heartland. Irrespective of the form of rent assessment, therefore, a *jagir* assignee who was not able to collect his rents in time faced the predicament of having to leave for Kumaun or other places on the western front with empty pockets.

The Gorkhali rulers made an attempt to solve the problem by granting authority to the *jagir* assignee to collect rents on an interim basis from cultivators. Such advance payments were euphemistically described as "loans" which were to be adjusted against the value of the rents after the crop was harvested. The rates of such advances ranged between 7.50 rupees and 15 rupees a *khet* depending on the yields, against the official value of 25 rupees, that is, between 30 percent and 60 percent.[24]

The system of collecting advance payments from the cultivator in this manner may have absolved the government of its liability, but did not mitigate the difficulties of the *jagir* assignees. This was so for two main reasons. In the first place, as payments fell into arrears, the *jagir* assignee remained saddled with the need for collecting the balance. Secondly, the advances were inadequate to meet his expenses in Kumaun or elsewhere on the western front. A soldier who was sent to the front from other parts of the region often had no more than 10 or 15 rupees in his pocket when he reached his destination.

Because of such tenurial diversities, the common denomination of *khet* in the *jagir* of a Gorkhali Company yielded different incomes in the two regions. In the trans-Bheri region, it yielded an income of 25 rupees in cash. In the heartland areas, because of various imponderable factors, such as yields and prices of agricultural produce, it is not possible to calculate the actual money value of the in-kind rents.

(4) Natural Disasters

Loss or damage of crops or lands resulting from such natural disasters as floods, landslides, drought, or hailstorms was yet another cause of the gap between the official value of *jagir* assignations and the actual income of the assignee. The rulers followed different policies in this respect in the heartland areas and the trans-Bheri region.

In the heartland areas, the 1796 royal order prescribing

the schedule of *jagir* assignations to armymen contained provisions for payment of compensation for losses caused by natural disasters. As previously noted, such compensation usually took the form of assignations of other rice-fields.[25] In December 1810, the practice of providing compensation for such losses was extended to Kumaun. That step was justified on the ground that "armymen cannot subsist unless they get their salaries".[26] Such a policy may have been justified in order to keep the Gorkhali armed forces intact, but it opened up the flood-gates for claims of compensation and, therefore, proved unpractical. About eight months later, in August 1811, Gorkhalis with *jagir* assignations in Kumaun were told:[27]

> Any shortfall in the sources of income assigned to any *jagirdar* as a result of famine, drought, depopulation, or floods and wash-outs, shall belong to the *jagirdar* himself. The loss of income resulting from depopulation shall not be realized from the existing households, but shall be shared equally.

This meant that once a *jagir* was assigned, the authorities considered their responsibility to have been fulfilled, and it was for the *jagirdar* and his company to collect what they could.

Power Without Responsibility

These is yet one more aspect to the problem. The *jagirs* of the army were assigned to the company, rather than to individual army men. The company sent its agents to make collections from the *thekbandi* holder in the concerned area or district. The sole object of the agents was "to exact as much as possible in the shortest time from their fields".[28] This gave rise to a confrontation between the faceless agents of the *jagirdar*-companies and the faceless representatives of the tax-paying peasants. It was a confrontation between power without responsibility and responsibility without power. Unauthorized collection and extortions from the peasants were the natural consequences of this unequal and impersonal relationship. The benefits of unauthorized collections belonged to the agents of the appropriate company, whereas losses due to incomplete collections or natural disasters fell on the concerned employees.

The judicial authority that *jagir* assignations placed in the hands of the *jagir* beneficiaries further complicated an already complex situation. In Kumaun, as in other provinces of the Gorkhali Empire, "the administration of justice was on no regular system, each of the officers exercising jurisdiction according to his position and the number of men at his disposal to ensure his orders being obeyed."[29] The administration of justice at the local level formed a part of the jurisdiction of the company, but no information is available about the manner in which such authority was actually exercised. But one thing is clear; the system did not ensure justice. In the absence of any regulation dealing with local disputes, or prescribing specific rates of fines and penalties, there was no alternative for the agents but to use their own discretion. It may be correct to assume that the emphasis was on income from fines and penalties, rather than on a fair trial and an impartial verdict.

The Two Ends

The *jagir* system followed by the Gorkhali rulers in Kumaun affected the two ends of the Gorkhali official spectrum, with *bhardars* at one end and the rank and file of the standing army, on the other, in quite different ways. The *jagir* scale of *bhardars* was quite high by Gorkhali standards, ranging between 3,600 rupees for a *sardar* and as much as 7,126 rupees for a *chautariya*. At the other end of the spectrum were the ordinary soldiers and auxiliaries of the army, whose *jagirs* ranged between 1.40 and 2 *khets*, the official income ranging between 35 rupees and 50 rupees a year. The *chautariya's jagir* of 7,126 rupees was thus 142 times higher than the *jagir* of a soldier. To be sure, such a wide disparity in the scale of official incomes is by no means a unique Gorkhali phenomenon, but can be seen in the hierarchies of any country in the world at any time in history. The disparity is also a reflection of the nature of official responsibility. No one can say that the *chautariya* and the soldiers must be compensated for their services with equal salaries.

The real point is rather the vulnerability or otherwise of the *jagir* beneficiary. As an economist might say, the marginal utility of money is smaller at the top level compared with incomes at the lower end of the spectrum. A 50-percent loss of *jagir* income would still leave the *chautariya* with an income of 3,263 rupees. In contrast, the man at the bottom would have no more than 17.50 or 25 rupees in similar circumstances. Irrespective of how the top echelons of the administration and the army fared, Gorkhali personnel in the lower ranks faced a real problem of subsistence.

NOTES

1. Nayaraj Pant, *et al.*, *Shri 5 Prithvi Narayana Shahako Upadesha* (Teachings of King Prithvi Narayan Shah), n.d. pp. 326-27.
2. H.H. Wilson, *A Glossary of Revenue and Judicial Terms and Useful Words Occurring in Official Documents Relating to the Administration of British India* (reprint of 1855 ed.), Delhi, Munshiram Manoharlal, 1978, p. 224.
3. Mahesh C. Regmi, *A Study in Nepali Economic History, 1768-1846*, 1971, pp. 209-10.
4. Royal instructions to Subba Nar Shah in Kumaun, Poush sudi 2, 1849 (December 1792), *RRC*, Vol. 5, p. 239.
5. For a detailed study of the *jagir* system, see Mahesh C. Regmi, *Land Tenure and Taxation in Nepal*, 1978 ed., pp. 452-501.
6. Royal instructions to Kaji Ambar Simha Thapa, Baisakh badi 1, 1861 (April 1804), *RRC*, Vol. 19, p. 175.
7. Royal order to Chautariya Bam Shah regarding monthly salaries of armymen in Kumaun, Shrawan badi 3, 1855 (July 1798), *RRC*, Vol. 52, pp. 29-30.
8. Royal instructions to Kaji Ritudhwaj Khawas for Kumaun, Jestha sudi 3, 1862 (May 1805), *RRC*, Vol. 20, p. 188.

9. Mahesh C. Regmi, *Land Tenure and Taxation in Nepal*, p. 468.
10. Mahesh C. Regmi, *Kings and Political Leaders of the Gorkhali Empire, 1768-1814*, 1995, pp. 50-51.
11. *Jagir* schedules for Gorkhali companies, Ashadh sudi 5, 1853 (June 1796), *RRC*, Vol. 5, pp. 319-22; do. Shrawan sudi 15, 1854 (July 1797), *RRC*, Vol. 25, pp. 515-27; also see No. 8 above.
12. do.
13. See No. 6 above.
14. Royal order to the Tara Prasad and other *paltans* regarding compensation for *jagir* assignations in Juhar, Marga sudi 1, 1870 (November 1813), *RRC*, Vol. 41, pp. 388-89; Royal order to Chautariya Bam Shah and Subba Hastadal Shah, Marga sudi 15, 1868 (November 1811), *RRC*, Vol. 40, p. 318; Royal order to personnel of companies which had been granted *jagir* assignations in Darma and Byas, Baisakh sudi 3, 1870 (April 1813), *RRC*, Vol. 41, pp. 257-58.
15. Appointment of Nar Shah as Subba of Kumaun, Poush sudi 2, 1849 (December 1792), *RRC*, Vol. 5, pp. 234-35.
16. *Jagir* assignation to Kaji Ambar Simha Thapa, Baisakh badi 9, 1867 (April 1810), *RRC*, Vol. 39, pp. 152-53.
17. Jagir assignations to Naya Sri Gorakh Company, Kartik badi 7, 1862 (October 1805), *RRC*, Vol. 19, pp. 323-24; Royal order to Subedar of Ramaban Company, Aswin sudi 9, 1867 (September 1810), *RRC*, Vol. 39, pp. 441-42; Royal order regarding *jagir* assignations of the Dalamardan Company, Aswin sudi 1, 1867 (September 1810), *RRC*, Vol. 39, pp. 417-18.
18. Colonel Kirkpatrick, *An Account of the Kingdom of Nepaul*, 1971 (reprint of 1811 ed.). pp. 98 and 108.
19. Royal proclamation regarding *jagir* assignations in the Gorkhali Empire, Ashadh sudi 5, 1850 (June 1793), *RRC*, Vol. 36, pp. 51-54.
20. See No. 11 above.

21. Royal order to the inhabitants of Bandipur, Mahibol, and other areas in Tanahu, Ashadh badi 7, 1865 (June 1808), *RRC*, Vol. 36, p. 118; do. to the village headmen of Dhading, Shrawan badi 9, 1864 (July 1807), *RRC*, Vol. 20, p. 471.

22. Mahesh C. Regmi, ***Thatched Huts ad Stucco Palaces, Peasants and Landlords in 19th-Century Nepal***, 1978, pp 55-7; Royal orders to peasants cultivating *jagir* lands of companies in Kaski, Nuwakot, and other districts, Ashadh badi 9, 1864 (June 1807), *RRC*, Vol. 20, p. 428-29; Royal order regarding crop-sharing on *jagir* lands in Timalkot and other areas, Kartik badi 1, 1862 (October 1805), *RRC*, Vol. 19, p. 288; Royal order regarding collection of *kut* rents in the Daraundi-Dhurkot region, Poush sudi 15, 1868 (January 1812), *RRC*, Vol. 40, p. 336.

23. Francis Buchanan Hamilton, *An Account of the Kingdom of Nepal*, 1971 (reprint of 1819 ed.), p. 211.

24. See No. 22 above.

25. See No. 11 above. Also see Royal order to the Durga Bux Company, Marga badi 3, 1862 (November 1805), *RRC*, Vol. 19, p. 395.

26. Royal order to Chautariya Bam Shah and Subba Hastadal Shah, Poush badi 10, 1867 (December 1810), *RRC*, Vol. 38, pp. 695-96.

27. Royal order to companies with *jagir* assignations in Kumaun, Bhadra badi 12, 1868 (August 1811), *RRC*, Vol. 40, pp. 253-54.

28. Atkinson, p. 628.

29. do. p. 626; Royal order to agents of companies with *jagir* assignations in Kumaun, Marga sudi 9, 1869 (November 1812), *RRC*, Vol. 41, pp. 475-76.

7

The Impact of Gorkhali Rule

At some very basic level, imperialism means thinking about, settling on, controlling land that you do not possess, that is distant, that is lived on and owned by others. For all kinds of reasons, it attracts some people and often involves untold misery for others.

Edward W. Said[1]

In 1815, when Gorkhali rule in Kumaun came to an end, the landscape was marked by "numerous waste villages" and "the incomplete state of agriculture which prevails generally in the villages still inhabited".[2] This is what the British sources say, and it is possible that there is some measure of exaggeration designed to set off the succeeding British administration in a favourable light. Such a conclusion, however, would be rather simplistic. The British observation confirms what the Gorkhali rulers themselves admitted numerous times throughout almost the entire period of their administration in Kumaun, a persistent decline of population. This chapter begins with an account of the impact of the Gorkhali conquest on the people of Kumaun, the exodus of population, and the reactions of the Gorkhali rulers.

A Traumatic Experience

In Kumaun, according to a British source, "all was confusion and despair when news of the Gorkhali invasion reached Almora".[3] A modern historian from Garhwal has similarly recorded:[4]

> Stories about the barbaric repression by the Gorkhalis had spread far and wide in the Himalayan region, causing fear, dismay, and panic in Almora and Srinagar and leading the local people to believe in the legend that saint Gorakhnath had granted a boon to the Gorkhali Kings that they would conquer all the hill-states of the region.

The Gorkhali conquest was a traumatic experience for the people of Kumaun, for it came in the midst of oppression and tyranny by the Chand rulers themselves. Indeed, according to a British source:[5]

> It mattered little to the working population which (faction) succeeded to the supreme power. The constant change of masters and the irregular demands which were found necessary to recruit an empty exchequer tended to weaken the tie of loyalty to those nominally possessed of the reins of government. This was the reason why the common people offered little opposition to the Gorkhali invaders.

For the people of Kumaun, the change of masters only meant jumping from the frying pan into the fire. If the Chands were oppressive rulers, the Gorkhali administrators of the province proved even more so. According to the same British source, "Though but little opposition had been shown by the people (of Kumaun) to their new masters, they were none the less harassed, taxed and oppressed by them".[6]

The Kathmandu-Almora contact was ominous from the very outset. It started with a campaign of pillage, a standard practice of the Gorkhalis in the territories conquered by them.[7] According to an 1810 royal order to Gorkhali authorities in the Bheri-Jamuna region, "loot and plunder take place in the year when any new territory is conquered".[8] In 1805, Gorkhali *bhardars* who were appointed as chief administrators of the trans-Sutlej states of Kullu, Sirmur, Handur, and Kangra were ordered to transmit to Kathmandu all "books, weapons, and other valuable objects found in the royal palaces of those states. They were also ordered to give special rewards to fighting men "who engage in loot and killings".[9] It would certainly be interesting to find out whether any artifact of Kumaun origin has had a place in the heirlooms of descendants of the Gorkhalis who were stationed in that province during the quarter-century of Gorkhali rule.

The Political Impact

The Gorkhali conquest of Kumaun was followed by the elimination of its traditional political elite groups. The defeated ruler, Mahendra Chand, and his uncle, Lal Singh, fled to the territories of the Nawab of Avadh. So did a large section of the traditional political elite. At the same time, several top-ranking political leaders of Kumaun collaborated with the Gorkhalis. They included Harsha Dev Joshi, leader of a powerful faction of the traditional political elite. He defected to the Gorkhali side in 1789 and entered Almora "in triumph" with the Gorkhalis in 1791. About one year later, however, Harsha Dev Joshi left the Gorkhali side because the Gorkhalis reneged on their promise to appoint him chief of the Gorkhali administration in Kumaun. He then became "a mortal enemy of Gorkhali rule".[10]

The Gorkhalis long expected both Lal Singh and Harsha Dev Joshi to join their side. During 1802-03, Gorkhali authorities in Kumaun received the following instructions from Kathmandu:[11]

> If Lal Singh and Harsha Dev Joshi are willing to come over to the Gorkhali side, provide them with land and other sources which will yield an income of 4,000 rupees and 3,000 rupees respectively every year. Keep their families in Kumaun and send those two persons to Kathmandu.

In April 1804, Harsha Dev Joshi was promised that he would be allowed possession of his lands if he worked loyally in the Gorkhali cause.[12] But neither leader succumbed to these overtures.

There were also several individuals and groups in Kumaun who affirmed their loyalty to the Gorkhalis in return for economic and other favours. For instance, in 1804, Padma Nidhi Tiwari, a Brahmin of Kumaun, was granted tax-free lands for having performed religious ceremonies at a local shrine to ensure the victory of the Gorkhalis.[13] Often such people, particularly Brahmins, defected because they feared that the Gorkhalis would confiscate land grants made by the Chand rulers.[14] In 1809-10, the Gorkhalis confiscated lands belonging to a number of Brahmins, including Padma Nidhi Tiwari, on the charge of having engaged in anti-Gorkhali activities. The charges were later found untrue, and their lands were restored to them.[15] But such incidents made it clear that non-collaboration with the Gorkhalis was a risky affair for those who had economic and other stakes in Kumaun.

Meanwhile, the exodus of population from Kumaun continued and even spread to other strata of the society. The new fugitives included revenue functionaries and other elite groups whose traditional role of local leadership had been sidelined by the Gorkhalis. In 1796, King Ran Bahadur made appeals to them to return home. He admitted that the provincial Gorkhali authorities had committed atrocities on the people, "who, out of fear, have abandoned their homes and lands and fled to other places." He then declared:[16]

> You had served the former king of Kumaun faithfully. By the grace of God, that territory now belongs to us. Good people should be loyal to the throne, rather than to any individual. Kumaun is your home. Come back to your home and do the work allotted to you by the local authorities. We pardon you for any offense you may have committed.

Ran Bahadur also called on the fugitives to serve the Gorkhali authorities in the same way as they had served the former rulers.

The Cultural Impact[17]

Reference has been made in the Prologue to the cultural

imperialism of the Gorkhali state in Kumaun, which was basically aimed at enforcing traditional Hindu customs and usages relating to caste, commensal relations, untouchability, and sexual relations. All such matters were brought under the control of the Gorkhali state and dealt with by the provincial Gorkhali authorities in the secular field, and by Brahmin authorities, called *dharmadhikar*, in the social and religious fields. The *dharmadhikar*, or his agents, granted expiation to people who violated the sanctions and strictures of orthodox Hinduism. The subject needs more intensive research than is possible in this volume. I shall here limit myself to a brief description of the Gorkhali policies in the social and religious life of the people of Kumaun.

The main offenses which were placed under the jurisdiction of the *dharmadhikar* were adultery with a relative or person belonging to the same clan, or with a Brahmin woman; association with people belonging to any untouchable caste, infanticide, murder of a person belonging to the same clan, suicide, poisoning, and cow slaughter. Other sanctions and strictures were as follows:

> People who commit any of the following offenses may be granted expiation and allowed to mix with others belonging to the same caste and take cooked rice from their hands: People who take food contaminated by the touch of a woman during her periods, Brahmins who draw the plow; people who take dry food from the hands of those belonging to a low caste, and sacred-thread-wearing people who keep chicken or take dry food from the hands of Magars and Gurungs, high-cast people who take water contaminated by the touch of a damai or sarki; or eat wheat or barley crushed by doms, share the pipe with them, or drink water carried by them with a layer of leaves underneath the pitcher (so as to avoid direct bodily contact).

Castes and communities who traditionally used the services of Brahmin priests in rituals connected with the birth-death cycle were forbidden to stop doing so. The *dharmadhikar* granted expiation on payment of fees at "reasonable" rates, of which he was allowed to appropriate one-seventh. The balance belonged to the central authorities.

Whatever may have been the aim of Gorkhali policies in the field of cultural imperialism, one thing is beyond doubt: Such policies increased the financial burden on the people of Kumaun. It is significant that with one or two exceptions, no specific rates were ever prescribed for such fees and fines. Kirkpatrick has recorded that "most offenses, according to the *Dharma Shaster* (which is the foundation of the civil code of (Nepaul) being punishable by amercement, and the catalogue of crimes of this description being extremely long, it is easy to conceive that such penalties constitute a considerable source of emolument." Consequently, he goes on to say, income from expiation fees was "very great". Hamilton has similarly recorded that such income had "enormously multiplied" under Gorkhali rule. The Gorkhali policies in the field of cultural imperialism in Kumaun accordingly provided new sources of income to the authorities, both secular and religious, at the cost of the people. They used the opportunities created through such policies to interfere in the personal lives of the people for their own benefit.

The Social Impact

Under the Gorkhalis, the people of Kumaun were treated as second class people, with the commonest Gorkhali soldier ranking higher than the respectable people of the province. In 1804, Kaji Ambar Simha Thapa, on his appointment as Chief of the provincial administration in Kumaun, was ordered to punish Gorkhali soldiers who enticed or abducted married women, and to restore the women to their husbands.[18] Such an order would not have been issued had the Gorkhalis not engaged in those malpractices. The order was never implemented. This was quite natural in view of the Kaji's preoccupation with the cares of war and territorial expansion. Indeed, he could hardly have spent any time and energy in tracking down and acting against the virile

Gorkhalis from the hills who enticed or abducted the women of Kumaun.

Meanwhile, the impact of Gorkhali rule on the society of Kumaun progressively worsened. In October 1810, the Bhandari-Khatri team was ordered to inflict severe punishment on armymen belonging to such traditionally low-status castes and communities as Khas, Magar, Khawas and Gurung who married Brahmin girls without any consideration of caste. It would seem inconceivable that the consent of either the girls or their parents was freely obtained for such inter-caste alliances in early 19th century Kumaun. Indeed, the instructions are a wholesale indictment of Gorkhali rule. Crimes for which the team was empowered to inflict punishment included "torture, abduction, and rape of the wives, daughters, and daughters-in-law of the people, collection of unwarranted payments, fines and penalties, forcible appropriation of property, and enslavement of children." The list is long and nauseating. However, such royal orders seem to have had little practical impact. Three years later, in December 1813, Kaji Bakhtawar Simha Basnyat was similarly ordered to punish men belonging to liquor-drinking castes from marrying girls belonging to the sacred-thread wearing castes by lying about their own caste status.[19]

Enslavement was another socio-economic problem that acquired serious proportions in Kumaun under the Gorkhali rule. The Gorkhalis did not create the problem, for slavery was then a traditional institution in almost all parts of the Himalayan region. The Gorkhalis were faced with the problem of large-scale and indiscriminate enslavement only after the conquest of territories situated west of the Bheri river. They found that in those territories no caste was immune from enslavement, not even those which claimed a high status in the local society such as Brahmin and Rajput. In October 1803, enslavement of Brahmins and Rajputs was banned all over the Empire.[20] In subsequent years, people belonging to such monastic orders as Jogi and Sanyasi were added to the list, while Rajputs were left out.[21]

The Gorkhali rulers initiated a series of steps with the objective of mitigating the adverse impact of slavery on the people. Kathmandu realized that "the country has been ruined because the local administrators take the wives, sons and daughters of the local people as slaves for themselves, or sell them in the plains" on the ground of non-payment of taxes.[22] Enslavement was also a form of punishment for people belonging to castes and communities who were not eligible to wear the sacred thread, a symbol of high ritual status under the four tier caste system of orthodox Hinduism, who indulged in extra-marital sexual relations. The practice was banned in 1812, and punishment was prescribed in the form of fines.[23] Forcible enslavement was also banned, although with the caveat that it would be permitted on the basis of mutual consent and endorsement by respectable people in the village.[24] In September 1808, the Gorkhali administrators in the provinces and vassal states of the western regions, including Kumaun, were told:[25]

> We have received complaints that the inhabitants of that province sell their children, or the children of others, to Muslims and other people from the plains, as well as to people from Tibet. Those who buy and sell children in this manner shall be severely punished.

About two years later, Gorkhalis in the Bheri-Jamuna region were ordered to bring back people who had been sold as slaves in the plains, the hill regions, the Himalayan region, or Kathmandu. Slave owners were ordered to surrender their slaves to the local Gorkhali authorities.[26] In 1813, Kaji Bakhtawar Simha Basnyat was ordered to inflict appropriate punishment on people who were guilty of such crimes as "enslavement of the sons and daughters of brahmins, sanyasis, and jogis, use force to compel people to sell their sons, daughters, and wives, engage in sexual relations with their daughters and daughters-in-law, or enslave people for default in land taxes and other payments, other than accepting slaves in payment of such taxes.[27]

These reform measures, however, remained limited to paper. In December 1814, soon after the Gorkha-Britain war began, another royal order admitted that "though the enslavement of children for non-payment of land taxes, and their slave as slaves, has been banned, the practice continues.[28]

The Gorkhali policy toward enslavement must, however, be taken in the proper perspective. As previously noted, slavery was a long-established practice in the region, and restrictions on enslavement were bound to prove ineffective so long as the demand for slaves continued. More than two decades after the end of Gorkhali rule, a British source has noted that in Kumaun, the purchase or temporary engagement of (slaves) for carrying on cultivation as well as the purchase of females for prostitution are still common and have never been prohibited".[29] Indeed, slavery and enslavement were legally banned in British India only in 1843.[30]

The Economic Impact

The Gorkhali conquest introduced a new element in the economy of Kumaun. It was comprised of people belonging to various strata in the administration, and the army, and their servants, porters, and bearers. Since there were no pack-animals, "all stores and supplies were carried by non-combatant camp servants. There were large numbers of them, for every soldier had his woman slaves and his "boy".[31] In addition, thousands of Gorkhali officers and employees travelled through Kumaun on their way to the front and also back to their homes in the heartland and other areas of the Empire. It is not possible to make a precise estimate of the two-way traffic. One can only say that the number of Gorkhalis at any given moment in the province, particularly after 1804, might be estimated in thousands. The pressure exerted by the Gorkhali presence on the food resources of Kumaun must accordingly have been enormous, even in conditions of normal production.

The Gorkhali rulers faced the problem of supplying food to the armed forces everywhere. Indeed, the problem was so chronic and acute that conscript troops were often told to bring their food along with them.[32] This, of course, was hardly a practical proposition. No man of the standing army was saddled with such an obligation.

The Gorkhali rulers adopted different solutions in different parts of the Empire to feed their troops. In the heartland and other areas, they often adopted the practice of compulsory procurement. For instance, in 1786, the landowners of Kaski were ordered to supply the prescribed quantity of rice to Gorkhali employees and troops stationed in Pokhara, and accept payments at rates fixed by the Gorkhali authorities.[33] During the Gorkha-Britain war, landowners in Parsa and other provinces in the Tarai region were ordered to supply rice on similar conditions to the military authorities in Hetauda.[34]

No such arrangements were made in Kumaun and other territories in the west. The Gorkhalis had, therefore, no alternative but to extort supplies from the local inhabitants under what was known as the *baikar* system. Together with the *begar* system, which was defined in Chapter 2 (Kathmandu and Almora) as forced labour services exacted in an unauthorized manner by Gorkhali officials and armymen for their own needs, the Gorkhali pressure on the society and economy of Kumaun was serious enough to lead to a massive exodus of population.

The problem had started soon after the Gorkhali occupation of Kumaun. In 1794, King Ran Bahadur referred to reports that "military personnel visit the villages and forcibly exact *baikar* from the people without making any payment." He decreed a ban on such requisitions, although legitimizing them" if the local authorities have issued orders in writing".[35] In 1804, Kaji Ambar Simha Thapa was ordered:[36]

(Gorkhali) officials and soldiers shall not loot goods in

> transit to the town, but shall purchase them on payment of the market price. Armymen shall not enter into the houses of the common people and demand money, and, if no money is paid, loot their goods.

In 1810, the Bhandari-Khatri team was similarly ordered:[37]

> Armymen travelling between Kathmandu and the front shall buy provisions from the people on payment of prices current in the area and with their consent. If they enter into the houses of the people and take away provisions by force, they shall be punished in the presence of the victims if they confess their guilt.

These exhortations remained limited to paper, for the Gorkhalis on the spot were a mere tangible force for the people of Kumaun than the central authorities if far-off Kathmandu.

A New Wave of Population Exodus

In December 1812 Kaji Bakhtawar Simha Basnet was ordered to make "suitable" arrangements for areas west of the Bheri river to check depopulation due to the indiscriminate and widespread use of the *begar* and *baiker* systems by the Gorkhalis.[38] Even as the Gorkha-Britain war began, the Gorkhali rulers continued their attempt to stem the population exodus. Indeed, an official team was appointed in November 1814 with instructions to bring back the emigrant population and resettle them in their lands and homes.[39] This was a desperate attempt to restore normal conditions and solve within a few weeks a problem that had defied solution for a quarter-century.

The situation reached a critical stage by the closing years of Gorkhali rule in Kumaun. Reports of the exodus of the local population because of *baikar* and *begar* exactions reached Kathmandu from almost all parts of the province.[40] The Gorkhali authorities were aware of the problem. However, they were powerless to introduce basic reforms in the administrative system of Kumaun. They only reiterated the ban on *baikar* and *begar* exactions, appealed to the fugitives to return to Kumaun, and sent men to persuade them to do so. However, the problem remained intractable. It was indeed futile for the Gorkhali rulers to repeat *ad infinitum* a ban which could not be enforced on the ground. The problem was built into the system of Gorkhali rule and so was only a symptom, rather than the disease itself.

Concluding Remarks

For the people of Kumaun, the 25 years long Gorkhali rule had a negative impact on important aspects of their lives, political, social, and economic. This was natural, for the Gorkhalis did not occupy Kumaun, and rule it for a quarter-century, for the benefit of its inhabitants. But the response of the people of Kumaun to the actions of the Gorkhali rulers was seldom one of confrontation or rebellion. It was rather marked by two alternative courses. The first course, which lay within the Gorkhali system itself, sought reforms through appeals and petitions to the central authorities in Kathmandu. The second alternative course was equally docile, for it took the form of resistance by voting with the feet and migrating to other territories. Resistance to the Gorkhali rule by such means was possibly more effective than the first course of action. How else can one explain the phenomenon of waste villages and the incomplete state of agriculture in Kumaun at the time of the British take-over?

NOTES

1. Edward W. Said, *Culture and Imperialism*, 1993, p. 7.
2. C.W. Traill, "Statistical Sketch of Kumaun," *Asiatic Research*, XVI (1829), p. 190, cited in L.F. Stiller, *The Rise of the House of Gorkha*, 1975, p. 267.
3. Atkinson, Edwin T., *The Himalayan Districts of the North-Western Provinces of India*, 1884, Vol. 2, p. 609.
4. Shiva Prasad Dabral, *Uttarakhanda Ka Rajnaitik Tatha Sanskritik Itihas* (Political and Cultural History of the Uttarakhanda region), 1973, pt. 5, pp. 63-64.

5. Atkinson, p. 623.

6. do.

7. Mahesh C. Regmi, *Kings and Political Leaders of the Gorkhali Empire, 1768-1814*, 1995, pp. 24-25.

8. Royal instructions to Kaji Bahadur Bhandari and Bakshi Dasharath Khatri for the Bheri-Jamuna region, Kartik badi 2, 1867 (October 1810), *RRC*, Vol. 39, p. 449.

9. Royal order to Kajis Ambar Thapa and Nayan Thapa for Kangra, Aswin sudi 2, 1862 (September 1805), *RRC*, Vol. 6, pp. 515-16. Similar orders were issued to Gorkhali *bhardars* in Kullu, Sirmur and Handur also on the same date, do, pp. 510-14.

10. Atkinson, pp. 590-609; Stiller, pp. 188-90, 223 and 358.

11. Royal instructions to Subba Rudravir Shah, Shrawan badi 8, 1859 (July 1802), *RRC*, Vol. 24, pp. 571-85.

12. Royal order to Harsha Dev Joshi, Chaitra sudi 11, 1860 (April 1804), *RRC*, Vol. 19, p. 181.

13. Royal order regarding *birta* grant to Padmanidhi Tiwari, Kartik sudi 11, 1867 (October 1810), *RRC*, Vol. 38, p. 604.

14. Royal orders reconfirming tax-free privileges of Gangaram Shastri, Baisakh badi 9, 1867 (April 1810), *RRC*, Vol. 39, p. 151; *Regmi Research Series*, Year 10, No. 5, May 1, 1978, p. 69.

15. Separate royal orders to Brahmin *birta*-owners in Kumaun, Kartik 10, 1867 (October 1810), *RRC*, Vol. 38, p. 580.

16. *Regmi Research Series*, Year 4, No. 4, April 1, 1972, p 61-4.

17. This section is based on the following sources: "The *Dharmadhikar*", *RRS*, Year 8, No. 1, January 1, 1976, p. 20; The role of the Dharmadhikar", *RRS*, Year 11, No. 9, September 1, 1979, pp. 136-39; Royal order to the inhabitants of the Kali-Sutlej region, Poush sudi 14, 1809 (January 1813), *RRC*, Vol. 41, pp. 226-8; Royal instructions to Subba Nar Shah, Poush sudi 2, 1849 (January 1793), *RRC*, Vol. 5, pp. 234-39. Appointment of *Dharmadhikari* in the Bheri-Garhwal region, Shrawan badi 5, 1854 (July

1797), *RRC*, Vol. 25, p. 547; to Kaji Bahadur Bhandari and Bakshi Dasharath Khatri, 1810, (No. 8 above) and Marga badi 8, 1868 (November 1810), *RRC*, Vol. 38 pp. 640-44; and to Kaji Bakhtawar Simha Basnyat, Poush sudi 12, 1869 (December 1812), *RRC*, Vol. 41, pp. 188-91; Colonel Kirkpatrick, *An Account of the Kingdom of Nepaul*, 1971), p. 201; Francis Buchanan Hamilton, *An Account of the Kingdom of Nepal*, 1971, p. 102.

18. Royal instructions to Kaji Ambar Simha Thapa for Kumaun, Baisakh badi 1, 1861 (April 1804), *RRC*, Vol. 19, pp. 174-80.

19. Royal instructions to the Bhandari-Khatri team in 1810 and to Kaji Bakhtawar Simha Basnyat in 1813, (See No. 17 above).

20. Royal order banning enslavement of Brahmins and Rajputs, Katrik badi 10, 1860 (October 1803), *RRC*, Vol. 19, pp. 137-38.

21. Royal instructions to Kaji Bakhtwar Simha Basnyat, 1813, See No. 17 above.

22. Royal order to Chautariya Bam Shah, Ashadh badi 10, 1864 (June 1807), *RRC*, Vol. 20, p. 404.

23. Royal orders to local authorities in Garhwal and other territories, Magh badi 12, 1868 (January 1812), *RRC*, Vol. 40, p. 349; and Baisakh sudi 4, 1869 (April 1812), *RRC*, Vol. 41, pp. 82-83.

24. See No. 20 above.

25. Ban on enslavement of children in Kumaun and other areas, Aswin badi 8, 1865 (September 1808), *RRC*, Vol. 36, pp. 164-66; "Documents on Slavery," *RRS*, Year 1, No. 2, December 1, 1969, pp. 44-5.

26. Royal orders to Kaji Bahadur Bhandari and Bakshi Dasharath Khatri, Marga badi 8, 1867 (November 1810), *RRC*, Vol. 38, p. 640; to Gorkhalis in the Bheri-Jamuna region, Poush badi 9, 1867 (December 1810), *RRC*, Vol. 38, p. 688.

27. See No. 21.

28. Royal order to Dittha Dhanbir Thapa for Garhwal and other territories, Poush badi 3, 1871 (December 1814), *RRC*, Vol. 41, p. 456.

29. Ram P. Srivastav, "Tribe-Caste Mobility in India," in Christoph Von Furer-Haimendorf (ed.), *Caste and Kin in Nepal, India, and Ceylon*, 1978, p. 181.

30. K.M. Munshi, *et al.*, (ed.), *The History and Culture of the Indian People, British Paramounty and Indian Renaissence*, Vol. X, Part II, p. 280, 1965.

31. John Pemble, *The Invasion of Nepal*, p. 29.

32. Royal proclamation on conscription in Kathmandu and other areas, Kartik sudi 14, 1871 (October 1814), *RRC*, Vol. 41, pp. 429-31.

33. Royal order to the landowners of Kaski, Ashadh sudi 8, 1843 (June 1786), *RRC*, Vol. 25, p. 159.

34. Royal orders to the landowners of Parsa, Kartik badi 4, 1872 (October 1815), *RRC*, Vol. 42, p. 91.

35. Royal order to local functionaries in Kumaun, Shrawan badi 8, 1851 (July 1794), *RRC*, Vol. 5, p. 183.

36. See No. 18 above.

37. See No. 8 above.

38. See No. 17 above.

39. Royal instructions to Najiki Nawal Simha and others for the Dharmathali-Besahar region, Marga badi 4, 1871 (November 1814) *RRC*, Vol. 41, p. 443.

40. Royal orders to local authorities in Chaugarkha, Baisakh sudi 2, 1869 (April 1812), *RRC*, Vol. 41, pp. 117-18, and Askoṭ, Kartik sudi 8, 1869 (October 1812), *RRC*, Vol. 41, pp. 131-32; and to Kaji Bakhtawar Simha Basnyat, Poush badi 14, 1869 (January 1813), *RRC*, Vol. 41, p. 192.

Epilogue

I shall write without indignation or partnership: in my case the customary incentives to these are lacking.

*Tacitus**

An attempt will be made here to recapitulate the main themes of the study and underline the principal factors that had a bearing on the working of Gorkhali imperialism in Kumaun.

The main point that emerges from the discussion is the fragile character of the Gorkhali Empire. The *dhungo* ideology of the Gorkhali rulers, to which reference has been made in the Prologue, was not sufficient to bind the subject populations of Kumaun and other colonial territories with the center. The reason was that the two sides lacked any common ties beyond those of domination and dependence. The absence of such ties became more and more marked as the Gorkhali Empire expanded over far-off territories and brought within its fold a variety of castes and communities. What benefited the Gorkhalis was not what benefited the subject populations of the conquered territories.

Prithvi Narayan Shah had faced up to only a few states in the Gorkhali heartland in the Cis-Marsyangdi region; his successors faced more numerous and stronger enemies in the trans-Marsyangdi region up to Kumaun and beyond. The Gorkhali state's strategic situation became weaker as the frontiers of the empire extended. The line of

* Publius Cornelius Tacitusi, The *Annals of Imperial Rome*, trans. by Michael Grant, Middlesex: Penguin Books, 1977, P. 32.

communication became longer, and far from contributing economic resources to the Gorkhali state, the newly-conquered territories actually absorbed the economic resources of the heartland and other more accessible territories.

The progressive weakening of the Gorkhali state was also due to the decline of the role of the King as the center-piece of the Gorkhali authority. Prithvi Narayan Shah had provided strong and active leadership in the political, administrative, military, and other fields, and on several occasions even took part in actual fighting. His successors were minors when they ascended the throne, or else were nonentities devoid of political understanding, with one of them, Ran Bahadur shah, casting a malignant influence on the fate of the Gorkhali state. His abdication, self-exile, and assassination emasculated the Gorkhali state beyond repair. Politics at the royal court in Kathmandu, the focal point of the empire, was thereafter marked by intrigue, slander, and even assassinations. The political elites, consequently, became demoralized and started giving greater attention to grabbing the spoils of office and enriching themselves and their families than to the interests of the Gorkhali state. They also adopted the strategy of strengthening their own leadership at the cost of the Gorkhali state by sending off their rivals, both actual and prospective, to fight a mindless campaign of expansion, particularly after 1804.

For the Gorkhali rulers, the conquest of Kumaun was not an end in itself. Rather, it was a means toward the fulfilment of their imperial ambitions. Kumaun and its people were needed only because they could be used as a base for further imperial conquests and a source of economic and manpower resources. They were treated as estates to be exploited for the imperial war effort, rather than to be protected and nurtured as integral parts of the Gorkhali empire. The Gorkhali occupation of Kumaun was only an episode in the general drama of Gorkha's imperial expansion.

Moreover, the economic resources mobilized by the Gorkhalis in Kumaun were spent mainly for sustaining the Gorkhali civil and military establishment in that province in the course of the imperial expansion. The policies followed by the Gorkhali rulers only effected a redistribution of resources for fulfilling their imperial design. They made no contribution toward increasing production and wealth. War, or preparations for war, always lead to an unproductive use of human and material resources. Nor was the scale of absorption of resources from the people of Kumaun matched by the contribution made by the Gorkhalis to their security and welfare.

The invidious practices of *baikar* and *begar* seem to have been the last straw on the backs of the people. Under these systems, any Gorkhali could intrude into the houses of the people, exact food and other supplies, and force people to carry loads and provide other labour services, all without wages or other compensation. One can easily imagine that such exactions were not limited to essential needs. Given the circumstances in which the Gorkhalis worked and travelled in Kumaun, they could hardly be expected to follow a self-denying code of conduct. Gorkhali armymen and other employees were granted a blank check on the inhabitants of the province, which they cashed to the maximum possible extent. But the Gorkhali cause was not the cause of the people of Kumaun.

In all fairness, one must admit that the central authorities did not condone the exaction of unauthorized payments and services by the provincial authorities or other Gorkhalis. Indeed, they issued orders from time to time banning such exactions as well as other abuses of Gorkhali rule. It would be unfair to doubt their concern for the plight of the workers and peasants of Kumaun. But pious intentions without the will or means to enforce them, or to live with the consequences of enforcement, are of no significance. For the Gorkhali rulers the campaign of imperial expansion was of overriding importance. If the campaign was to be carried forward, the manpower and other resources of the Empire would have to be exploited to the utmost limit, and if, in the process, certain abuses were unavoidable, then so be it. It is on these lines that the Gorkhali mind at the central level seems to have worked. Accordingly, one can discern a note of hypocrisy in orders imposing a ban on unauthorized collections, as well as on *baikar* and *begar* exactions repeatedly in an almost ritualistic fashion. Ineffective administrative control may have hampered the actual enforcement of the ban, but one is left with a lurking suspicion that it was never meant to be enforced. *Baikar* and *begar* constituted the bedrock sustaining the Gorkhali war, it effort in the provinces, in the same way as the *jhara* system sustained the Gorkhali infrastructure at the state and local levels.

The real intentions of the Gorkhali leaders had at least two manifestations. Firstly, they had a tolerant attitude toward earring *bhardars* short of dismissing or transferring them; or reminding them that the collection of unauthorized payments is a sin. Such appeals to the conscience of the provincial Gorkhali authorities only reveal the ineffective character of Gorkhali policies.

In the prologue, I had promised to explain in the Epilogue my stand on the controversy about the nature of Gorkhali imperial rule in Kumaun. Readers who have understood my ground plan for the study must already have had an inkling of my conclusions. On the basis of the evidence I have presented in these pages, I have no hesitation in arriving at the conclusion that the Gorkhali rule in Kumaun was congenitally marked by such malpractices as "extraction, torture, abduction and rape of the wives, daughters, and daughters-in-law of the people, collection of unwarranted payments, fines and penalties, forcible appropriation of property, and enslavement," and that the people of that province suffered great hardships and miseries in all aspects of life. The evidence certainly does not show that "the Gorkhalis were commanding a great support from the general population" of Kumaun. Rather, it substantiates the British view, although somewhat exaggerated, that, "nothing could exceed the hatred which the tyranny of twenty-five years had created." It will be wrong to attribute such an attitude of the people of Kumaun to specific mistakes by the Gorkhali authorities, rather than to the inherent defects of Gorkhali rule.

This conclusion should by no means be construed as a moral indictment of the Gorkhali rule in Kumaun. The historian's task is to analyze and interpret the events of the past from the vantage-point of the present. Accordingly, a moral posture lies outside his scope. Human misery has been an integral feature of human history through the millennia and the progress of one nation or group has mostly been at the cost of another, and the Gorkha-Kumaun case was no exception. In any case, the *dramatis personae* of this account are all dead, so any moral condemnation of approbation of their actions would be an exercise in futility. It is only the consequences of their actions that remain relevant today, and that is what I have tried to show in this volume.

Glossary

Baikar	—Requisitioning of food and other provisions from local households without any payment.
Begar	—Unpaid porterage and other labour services exacted by individuals.
Bhardar	—A high-ranking Gorkhali officer.
Birta	—Tax-free and inheritable land grants made by the state to individuals.
Chautariya	—A royal advisor or regent belonging to the ruling Shah family.
Darmahadar	—Armymen who were paid salaries in cash.
Dhungo	—Literally, a stone; metaphorically, the Gorkhali state.
Guthi	—Land and other sources of revenue endowed by the state or by individuals to finance religious or charitable functions.
Hulak	—A system under which official mail or supplies were transported by relays of porters impressed from among the local peasantry.
Ijara	—A revenue-farming assignment.
Jagir	—Lands, homesteads, villages and other sources of revenue assigned to government employees as remuneration for their services.
Jhara	—Unpaid labour exacted by the government on a compulsory basis.
Kaji	—A minister-level *bhardar*.
Khet	—(a) Irrigated lands in the hill region on

which rice and wheat are grown.

—(b) A measure of rice-lands in the hill region equal to 25 *ropanis* or 100 *muris* (approximately 1.25 hectare).

Khuwa —Hill-side villages and settlements which yielded revenue in cash as part of *jagir* assignations.

Kut —A system of share-cropping in the central hill region under which the cultivator paid a fixed quantity of produce, or a fixed amount of money, as rent.

Kusahi-Bisahi —A one-time levy on *birta* owners.

Lajima —Auxiliary or non-combatant personnel in a Gorkhali Company.

Majhi —A ferryman or fisherman.

Mukhtiyar —A regent or viceroy.

Nal —Combatant personnel of a Gorkhali company.

Pajani —A system under which government employees of all categories were screened every year and dismissed, reappointed, or promoted.

Praja —Castes or communities whose members were not eligible for military service.

Raikar —State-owned lands from which the government collected rents or taxes.

Rupee —A unit of account which was comprised of between 12 and 20 *annas*; an *anna* was equivalent to 4 *paisa* coins.

Sardar —A civil or military officer of *bhardar* rank.

Subba —Chief of the provincial administration.

Subedar —Commander of a Gorkhali company.

Thekbandi —A system under which the amount of taxes and other payments was assessed for a district, village, or other area in a lump sum payable on an annual basis.

Appendices

Appendix A

THE GORKHALI KINGS (1742-1816)

1. *King Prithvi Narayan Shah* (1742-75) of Gorkha shifted his capital to Kathmandu in September 1768. He died on January 10, 1775 at the age of 52.

2. *Pratap Simha Shah* (1775-77) : Succeeded to the throne on the death of his father, Prithvi Narayan Shah; died on November 17, 1777.

3. *Ran Bahadur Shah* (1777-99) : Succeeded to the throne at the age of 16 months on the death of his father, Pratap Simha Shah. Regents : Queen-Mother Rajendra Laxmi and Bahadur Shah, Prithvi Narayan Shah's younger son (1777-79), Rajendra Laxmi (1779-85) and Bahadur Shah (1785-94). In April 1794, Ran Bahadur removed the Regent, Bahadur Shah, and took over the administration.

4. *Girban Yuddha Bikram* (1799-1816) : On March 8, 1799, Ran Bahadur abdicated in favour of his son, Girban Yuddha Bikram, who was then 18 months of age. Regents : Queen Subarna Prabha (1800-3), Queen Rajrajeshwari Devi (1803-4), Ex-King Ran Bahadur Shah (1804-6) (assassinated in early 1806). Queen Lalit Tripura Sundari along with Kaji, later *mukhtiyar* and General, Bhimsen Thapa (1806-37), Girban died on November 20, 1816 at the age of 18.

Appendix B

RULERS OF KUMAUN, 1726-91

Ajit Chand	-	1726-30
Kalyan Chand	-	1730-47
Dip Chand	-	1748-77
Mohan Chand	-	1777-79, 1786-88
Pradyumna	-	1779-86
Shiv Chand	-	1788
Mahindra Chand	-	1788-91

The following accound of the political vicissimke suffered by Kumaun is based on Edwin T. Atkinson, *The Himalayan Districts of the North-Western Provinces of India*, Allahabad, 1882, Vol. II, pp. 582-606.

In 1726, Kumaun's ruler Devi Chand, "A weak and irresolute prince and altogether in the hands of the advisers in power for the time being," was assassinated "at the instigation of his "treacherous" ministers. They then installed a distant relative named Ajit Singh, on the throne of Kumaun with the name of Ajit Chand. The story was repeated about three years later. Ajit Chand was assassinated, and the victorious faction chose a distant relative in Doti who was "living in great poverty and reduced almost to toll the ground with his own hands for a subsistence", with the name of Kalyan Chand. His bloody, despotic and vindicative" rule came to an end with his death in 1748. His son, Dip Chand, succeeded him. He was "a man of mild, weak temperament, generous and kind to a fault", "entirely is the hands of the priests," and "practically ruled by whichever party should succeed in obtaining the nominal office of Diwan." Meanwhile, Mohan Singh, "the spuriously descended cousin" of Dip Chand, entered into the murky political scene of Kumaun, initially appointed as *bakshi* or head of the army, he eventually "established himself as head of the government". In 1777, he imprisoned the ruler, Dip Chand, who later died in suspicious circumstances. Mohan Singh then "proclaimed himself Raja under the title of Mohan Chand, and assumed all the insignia of a rightful ruler at his installation". However, he unleashed "a complete reign of terror" in Kumaun. The rulers of both Doti and Garhwal intervened, and Mohan Chand fled to the Rohilla capital of Rampur in the South.

The invaders then installed Pradyumna Shah, a son of the ruler of Garhwal, on the throne of Kumaun under the title of Pradyumna Chand. This arrangements came to an end about seven years later, in 1786, when Pradyumna's father, Raja Lalit Shah, died, and he chose the throne of Garhwal rather than that of Kumaun.

Mohan Chand, who had long been trying to regain the throne of Kumaun, finally succeeded in stepping into the vacuum created by the return of Pradyumna to Garhwal. About three years later, he suffered a defeat at the hands of another faction, and was assassinated. His son, Mahindra Singh, fled to Rampur. The victorious faction then chose one Shiv Singh as ruler of Kumaun with the name of Shiv Chand. But his tenure was brief. Within a few months, Mahindra Singh, a Son of Mohan Chand, occupied the throne with the help of Garhwal. He was the last independent ruler of Kumaun, for the state was annexed by the Gorkhalis early in 1791.

Bibliography

The records of the Department of Land Revenue in the Finance Ministry of His Majesty's Government of Nepal have provided the main source materials for this study. Copies of these materials are in the personal possession of the author in the form of the *Regmi Research Collection* (RRC). These sources have been cited at appropriate places in the notes, but are not individually listed in this. Published materials in the English, Nepali, and Hindi languages used in this study are listed below :

A English

Aitchison, C.V., *A Collection of Treaties, Engagements and Sunnuds Relating to India and Neighbouring Countries*, Calcutta: Bengal Printing Company Limited, 1863.

Atkinson, Edwin, T. *The Himalayan Districts of the North-Western Provinces of India*, Allahabad: North-Western Provinces and Oudh Government Press, 1882.

Baden-Powell, *The Land Systems of British India*, Delhi: Oriental Publishers, 1974 (reprint of 1892 ed.), 3 Vols.

Bagley, J.J., *Historical Interpretation, Sources of English Medieval History, 1066-1540*, Middlesex, Penguin Books, 1965.

Bista, Dor Bahadur, *The People of Nepal*, Kathmandu, Department of Publicity, HMG, 1967.

(British) Ministry of Defense, *Nepal and the Gurkhas*, London: HM"s Stationery Office, 1965.

Brown, D. Mackenzie, *The White Umbrella: Indian Political Thought From Manu to Gandhi*, Bombay: Jaico Publishing House, 1964.

Carr. E.H., *What is History ?*, Middlesex: Penguin Books, 1975.

Couch, Carl J., *Constructing Civilizations*, Connecticut: Jai Press Inc., 1984.

Encyclopaedia of the Social Sciences, New York: Macmillan, 1963.

Gibbon, Edward, *The Decline and Fall of the Roman Empire* (A one-volume abridgement by Dero A. Saunders), Middlesex Penguin Books, 1981.

Guha, Ram Chandra, *The Unquiet Woods*, New Delhi : Oxford University Press, 1989.

Hamilton, Francis Buchanan, *An Account of the Kingdom of Nepal* (reprint of 1819 ed.), New Delhi, Manjusri Publishing House, 1971.

Hamal, Lakshman B., *Military History of Nepal*, Kathmandu: Sharada Pustak Mandir, 1995.

Haimendorf, Christoph Von Furer (ed), *Caste and Kin in Nepal, India & Ceylon*, New Delhi: Sterling Publishers, 1978.

....., *Asian Highland Societies*, New Delhi, Sterling Publishers, 1981.

Khanal, Yadunath. *Nepal After Democratic Restoration*, Kathmandu: Ratna Pustak Bhandar, 1996.

Kirkpatrick, Colonel (William), *An Account of the Kingdom of Nepaul* (reprint of 1811 ed.), New Delhi: Manjusri Publishing House, 1969.

Landon, Perceval, *Nepal* (reprint of 1928 ed.), Kathmandu: Ratna Pustak Bhandar, 1978.

Marxism, Communism and Western Society: A Comparative Encyclopedia, New York, Herder and Herder, 1972, 8 Vol.

Morrall, John B., *The Medieval Imprint*, Middelesex: Penguin Books, 1967.

Munshi, K.M. *et al.*, (ed), *The History and Culture of the Indian People, British Paramountcy and Indian Renaissance*, Bombay: Bharatiya Vidya Bhavan, 1965.

Pant, S.D., *The Social Economy of the Himalayans*, London, George Allen and Unwin, 1935.

Pemble, John, *The Invasion of Nepal*, Oxford: Clarendon Press, 1971.

Regmi, D.R., *Modern Nepal*, Calcutta: Firma K.L. Mukhopadhyay, 1961.

Regmi, Mahesh C., *Land Tenure and Taxation in Nepal* (repint of 4-

volume 1963-68 ed.), Kathmandu: Ratna Pustak Bhandar, 1978.

——, *A Study in Nepali Economic History, 1768-1846* (reprint of 1971 ed.), Delhi : Adroit Publishers, 1978.

——, *Thatched Huts and Stucco Palaces: Peasants and Landlords in 19th Century Nepal*, New Delhi: Vikas Publishing House Pvt. Ltd., 1978.

——, *Readings in Nepali Economic History*, Varanasi: Kishor Vidya Niketan, 1979.

——, *The State and Economic Surplus*, Varanasi: Nath Publishing House, 1984.

——, *An Economic History of Nepal, 1846-1901*, Varanasi: Nath Publishing House, 1988.

——, *Kings and Political leaders of the Gorkhali Empire, 1768-1814*, Hyderabad: Orient Longman, 1995.

Rose, Leo E., *Nepal: Strategy for Survival*, Bombay, Oxford University Press, 1971.

Said, Edward W., *Culture and Imperialism*, New York, Vintage Books, 1993.

Spear, Percival, *A History of India*, Middlesex: Penguin Books, 1973.

Stilier, L.F., *The Rise of the House of Gorkha*, Kathmandu: Ratna Pustak Bhandar, 1975.

Tacitus, *The Annals of Imperial Rome*, trans, by Michael Grant, Middlesex: Penguin Books, 1977 (reprint).

Trevelyan, G.M., *English Social History*, London: Longmans, Green and Co. Ltd., 1952 ed.

Toynbee, Arnold J., *A Study of History*, (A 2-volume abridgement by D.C. Somervell), New York, Dell Publishing Co. Inc., 1974.

Wilson, H.H., *A Glossary of Revenue and Judicial Terms and Useful Words Occurring in Official Documents Relating to the Administration of British India* (reprint of 1855 ed.), Delhi: Munshiram Manoharlal, 1978.

B. Nepali

Acharya, Baburam, *Shri 5 Badamaharajdhiraja Prithvi Narayana Shah* (The Great King Prithvi Narayan Shah), Kathmandu: His

Majesty's Press Secretariat, Royal Palace, 2024-26 (1967-1969), 4 pts.

——, *Nepalako Samkshipta Vrittanta* (A concise account of Nepal), Kathmandu: Pramod Shumshere and Nir Bir Bikram "Pyasi", 2022 (1966).

Adhikari, Suryamani, *Paschim Nepalako Aitihasika Anweshana* (Historical exploration of western Nepal), Kathmandu: Center for Nepal and Asian Studies, 2043, (1986).

Gorkhapatra Chhapakhana, *Muluki Ain* (Legal Code), Kathmandu, 2012 (1955), pt 5.

Naraharinath, Yogi (ed), *Itihasa Prakasha* (Light on History), Kathmandu: Itihasa Prakasha Mandala, 2012-13 (1955-56), 4 Vols.

——, *Gorakha Vamshavali* (Genealogy of Gorkha), Varanasi, Aryabirasanga, 2021 (1964).

——, *Sandhipatra Sangraha* (A collection of treaties and documents), Dang: the editor, 2022 (1966).

Nepali, Chittaranjan, *Janaral Bhimsena Thapa ra Tatkalina Nepal* (General Bhimsen Thapa and contemporary Nepal), Kathmandu: Nepal Samskritik Sangh, 2013 (1956).

——, *Shri 5 Rana Bahadur Shah* (King Ran Bahadur Shah), Kathmandu, Mrs. Mary Rajbhandari, 2020 (1963).

Panta, Dinesh Raj, *Gorakhako Itihasa* (A history of Gorkha), Kathmandu, the author, 2041-43 (1985-86), 4 Vols.

Panta, Naya Raj, *et. al., Shri 5 Prithivinarayana Shahako Upadesha* (Teachings of King Prithvi Narayan Shah), Lalitpur: Jagadamba Prakashan, n.d., 4 Vols.

Sharma, Shiva Prasad, *et al., Nepalako Sainika Itihasa* (Military history of Nepal), Kathmandu: Royal Nepal Army Headquarters, 2049 (1992).

Shrestha, Tek Bahadur, *Parvatarajyako Aitihasika Ruprekha* (An historical outline of the Kingdom of Parbat), Kirtipur: Center for Nepal and Asian Studies, 2042 (1985).

C. Hindi

Dabral, Shiva Prasad, *Uttarakhanda Ka Rajanaitika Tatha Sanskritika*

Itihasa (Political and cultural history of the Uttarakhanda region), Garhwal, Bira Gatha Prakashana, 2030 (1973).

Pande, Badri Datta, *Kumaun Ka Itihasa* (History of Kumaun), Almora: Shyam Prakashan, 1990 (reprint).

Sankrityayan, Mahapandit Rahul, *Kumaun,* Varanasi: Gyanamandal, 2015 (1958).

Journals

Purnima, Nepali, quarterly, published by the Itihasa-Samshodhana Mandala, Kathmandu.

Regmi Research Series, (mimeo), English, monthly, published by the Regmi Research (P) Ltd. from November 1969 to December 1989.

Index

G

H

I

J

K

L

M

T

U

V

W